MADE
WITH
LOVE

CULINARY INSPIRATIONS FROM
AROUND THE WORLD

www.mascotbooks.com

Made With Love: Culinary Inspirations from Around the World

Editor: Virginia Lee
Photographer and Book Design: Warren East

For more information, please contact:
Mascot Books
620 Herndon Parkway #320
Herndon, VA 20170
info@mascotbooks.com

Library of Congress Control Number: 2020911933

CPSIA Code: PRTWP0920A
ISBN-13: 978-1-64543-579-2

Printed in Malaysia

To my husband Warren East and my mother and mentor, Virginia Lee.
Without your hard work, support and dedication, this book would
not have been possible.

To my father Mel Lee and my siblings, Katie and David;
thank you for all of your love and support.

To Robert & Stacey Lewis for being so awesome.

With deep gratitude to Gaby Hahn
and
In loving memory of
Nicky Hahn.

CONTENTS

FOREWORDS

There is nothing so serene as a Bahamian sunset, anchored off a picturesque, abandoned island, watching the turqoise waters and endless blue sky both turn to rose. A glass of cool white wine reflects the shimmering water. It is possible almost to be jaded by an endless succession of these, but what stands without compare is the dinner bell signaling another of Chef Elizabeth's creations.

Her innumerable awards don't do justice to what she can perform with a sous vide, a smoke gun, a droplet infuser, and sheer talent. That this can be performed with perfect presentation for weeks on end with a boat's physical restrictions is nothing short of extraordinary.

A day spent putting on a Robinson Crusoe impression, exploring deserted beaches, snorkeling with the sea turtles, and feeding bemused iguanas is perfectly ended by that bell ringing and the anticipation of what she might surprise us with next.

My heartfelt cheers to the greatest chef I've met on water and terra firma,

Philip Hahn

There are very few invitations in this life that are impossible to turn down. For most occasions, there will be an acceptable excuse if one does not wish to be sociable or if one has something better to do. But when it comes to an invitation to spend a week on board a yacht in the waters around the Bahamas, at just the right time of year, it is difficult to see how anybody could ever say no. And such invitations belong to another category too: those that require less than a minute's thought before acceptance. So when my wife and I received an invitation from Caroline Hahn to join her, her husband Richard, and her brother, Philip, on *Pegasus IX,* we accepted with unseemly alacrity.

I had expected comfort on *Pegasus IX,* and indeed the yacht has been so designed as to make everybody feel perfectly comfortable. As a sailor on lesser yachts, I was accustomed to limited space and making do. There was no need for any of that on this well-appointed vessel. I had also expected to be well-looked after: our hostess, Caroline, knows how to make guests feel welcome. But what I had no advance inkling of was the stunning cuisine to which we were treated during that week, and that, of course, was down to Elizabeth Lee, the chef who has now so generously decided to share her quite exceptional knowledge with the rest of us. And here we have it–in this marvellous volume with its well-explained and beautifully clear recipes.

For a week we were treated to many of the delights listed in these pages. Every meal was a work of art – from breakfast, with the morning sun sparkling on the water, through lunch, anchored somewhere before the afternoon siesta, to dinner with the sky above filled with white fields of stars. What could be a more perfect setting for culinary perfection? If heaven exists, then it might be something like this, with somebody like Elizabeth in charge of the catering.

I was writing at the time, working on a novel that has since been published. I am sure that if the novel has any quality to it, then that will be down, in large part, to the satisfied state of mind in which I wrote it. And that state of mind attributable, in turn, to Elizabeth's memorable meals, all served with the care and style that is the hallmark of a truly great chef.

I may have been working on a novel, but I also wrote a poem on board–a sonnet to *Pegasus IX.* The first letter of each line reads PEGASUS IX. This is the text:

Pegasus IX – **a sonnet**

Pegasus volans, white, a steed with wings,
Exempt from stasis, two-hulled, ex-ferry boat,
Goes in grace, conquers waves afloat;
A sailor forgets the land, puts aside those things
Salt and foam eschew; into a South-Easter
Under a cloudy sky, warm trades gusty,
Sending white wake astern, engines trusty,
Innocent of worries, only concerned lest
X on a chart conceals coral; on brine
Carpe diem, Latin advice, yet apt,
How can we forget: Chronos may be lapped,
The cautious, though, repeat: no one conquers time.
How right they are, but I confess:
Relaxing with friends, cares weigh rather less.

The poem is dedicated to the author of this book, this chef extraordinaire, this worker of culinary magic–with appreciation.

Alexander McCall Smith

WINES

Located in California's Monterey County, Hahn Family Wines is one of the first, largest, and most established winegrowers in the Santa Lucia Highlands. Founded 40 years ago by Nicolaus "Nicky" and Gaby Hahn, this family-owned California winery is renowned for its six certified sustainable estate vineyards and highly acclaimed wines.

From the start, Nicky realized that this mountainous region in Monterey County had every element vital to growing premium wine grapes: alluvial soils with excellent drainage, plenty of sunshine to develop rich, ripe fruit, and enough fog and wind to keep grape acids in perfect harmony. He recognized the area's potential as a world-class wine growing region and committed to producing distinctive wines worthy of competition on a global scale.

In 1988, Nicky pushed to define the unique attributes and boundaries of the Santa Lucia Highlands, and in 1991 his hard work paid off; the region was established as an official American Viticulture Area (AVA). Throughout the 1990s, the Hahns continued to innovate and invest in their vineyards and winemaking facility. Understanding that the cool growing climate of the Santa Lucia Highlands was ideally suited for native Burgundy varietals Pinot Noir and Chardonnay, the Hahns replanted existing estate vineyards and purchased SLH vineyards, Lone Oak, and Doctor's, as well as nearby Arroyo Seco vineyards, Ste. Philippe and Ste. Nicolas.

Hahn Family Wines employs sustainable farming practices and was one of the first Santa Lucia Highlands wineries to have all estate vineyards earn SIP certification (Sustainability in Practice). Sustainable farming is more than adapting sensible practices that save water, conserve soil, cut down on energy consumption, and reduce use of pesticides and other chemicals. It is a never-ending quest, a way of looking long-term, past the span of our own lives, to make decisions that not only pay off today but will be of benefit for generations to come. In every phase of grape growing and winemaking, Hahn Family Wines is committed to sustainable practices to promote healthy vineyards, satisfied consumers, and employee well-being.

Today, second-generation vintner Philip Hahn and his sister Caroline are at the helm, managing Hahn Family Wines. With more than 1,100 vineyard acres, ranging in elevation from 200 to 1,200 feet, they produce a portfolio of critically acclaimed estate-driven wines to suit any budget and tantalize every palate. The portfolio of brands includes Hahn, Hahn Estate, Hahn SLH, Lucienne, Smith & Hook, and Boneshaker. Several of these exceptional wines are paired with recipes in this book.

HAHN WINE TASTING NOTES

Hahn GSM
Enticing aromas of strawberry, black cherry, white pepper, and cinnamon. On the palate, notes of raspberry, a hint of cinnamon spice, along with strawberry and black cherry. Finishing with a smooth and luscious mouthfeel.

Hahn Pinot Noir
This wine's bouquet charms with scents of vibrant red cherry, red plum, and hints of spices with slightly toasty notes. On the palate, medium silky tannins with a soft, round mouthfeel and notes of earthiness.

Hahn SLH Pinot Noir
Aromas of red cherry and strawberry with hints of earth, spices, and toasty oak. An explosion of red fruit including strawberry, cherry, and raspberry welcome the palate and finish with refined tannins and a soft mouthfeel.

Smith & Hook Proprietary Red Blend
Opulent aromas of black currant, plums, and blueberry pie greet the nose, accompanied by hints of tobacco and leather. The refined yet robust palate is multidimensional, showcasing flavors of dark berries and vanilla, complemented by velveteen gripping tannins, a savory, richly dense mouthfeel and lingering finish.

Smith & Hook Cabernet Sauvignon
Vibrant aromas of dark fruit with hints of mocha, coffee, and toasty oak. Full bodied and rich with flavors of ripe plum and black cherry, the wine has a round, viscous mouthfeel backed with concentrated tannic structure that carries through to a smooth finish.

Lucienne Doctor's Vineyard Pinot Noir
The dry and slightly warmer climate here results in a riper, more robust Pinot Noir with layers of cherry and citrus fruits along with brown spice and tones of mushroom and earth. The wine's balanced acidity and smooth tannins lead to a round, approachably soft mouthfeel and a lingering finish.

Lucienne Smith Vineyard Pinot Noir
Lucienne Smith Pinot Noir features notes of raspberry, cherry, vanilla, and toast carrying through to sweet spice flavors on the palate. Soft yet structured, the wine is bright and fresh with medium acidity and a smooth finish.

Lucienne Lone Oak Pinot Noir
Just 20 acres of Lone Oak are devoted to Pinot Noir, creating an intensely aromatic wine with notes of citrus, cherry pie, toast, spice, and a hint of earthiness. The complexity continues on the palate with sleek cherry flavors, youthful balance, a round, soft texture and a long, structured finish.

Hahn Pinot Gris
Beautiful golden color with aromas of pear, citrus, lime, river stones, creamy melon, and grassy minerality. A thick and viscous mouthfeel is accompanied by flavors of tropical fruits, citrus, and hints of lemon blossom, finishing with bright acidity.

Hahn Chardonnay
Aromas of pineapple, lemon zest, and toasty vanilla. Bright acidity welcomes the palate, leading to a perfect balance of tropical fruit and subtle vanilla toast flavors that culminate in a lingering, clean finish.

Hahn SLH Chardonnay
Hahn SLH Chardonnay greets the nose with citrus, stone fruit, and hints of banana and vanilla. A viscous mouthfeel and medium acidity with hints of pear and vanilla.

Salads

Deconstructed Niçoise Salad
Flash-seared sashimi-grade tuna paired with new potato
salad, egg, organic greens, olive tapenade, caper
herb cream cheese, and crostini
Wine Pairing: Smith & Hook Proprietary Red Blend

Duck Confit Lyonnaise Salad
Paired with soft boiled egg, frisée, green beans, bacon
vinaigrette, and coral tuile
Wine Pairings: Lucienne Smith Vineyard Pinot Noir
or Hahn GSM

Lobster Salad
Poached lobster tail with baby potatoes, caramelized onions,
chorizo, peas, organic greens, and Parmesan tuiles
Wine Pairings: Lucienne Lone Oak Vineyard Pinot Noir
or Hahn SLH Chardonnay

Seared Shrimp Salad
With white wine and cream reduction, quinoa pilaf, organic
greens, cucumber, cherry tomatoes, and feta crumble
Wine Pairing: Hahn Pinot Gris

Sous Vide Grilled Skirt Steak Salad
With oven-dried cherry tomatoes, grilled vegetables, porcini
couscous, and blue cheese dressing
Wine Pairings: Smith & Hook Cabernet Sauvignon
or Lucienne Doctor's Vineyard Pinot Noir

Appetizers

Cheese

Caprese Salad
With heirloom tomatoes, buffalo mozzarella, pesto, balsamic
vinegar pearls, and glaze
Wine Pairing: Hahn SLH Chardonnay

Goat Cheese Soufflé
Paired with finger crostini, fresh herbs, and balsamic glaze
Wine Pairing: Hahn SLH Chardonnay

Italian Sushi
Grilled vegetables, prosciutto, herb cream cheese, cucumber,
tomato, and organic greens
Wine Pairing: Hahn Pinot Noir

Seared Hellim Bruschetta
Vine-ripened tomatoes on seared hellim with crostini and
micro greens
Wine Pairing: Hahn SLH Chardonnay

Meat

Duck Confit
With lentil rissoles, citrus gremolata, Hahn GSM onion
chutney, cilantro, and butter lettuce
Wine Pairings: Lucienne Lone Oak Vineyard Pinot Noir
or Hahn GSM

Sous Vide Beef Carpaccio
Thinly sliced beef with fragrance vegetables, frisée, shaved
Parmesan, and lemon oil
Wine Pairing: Lucienne Smith Vineyard Pinot Noir

Sous Vide Foie Gras
Paired with brioche toast points, Hahn red wine reduction,
and Hahn GSM onion chutney
Wine Pairing: Lucienne Doctor's Vineyard Pinot Noir

Appetizers

Seafood

Coconut Mahi Mahi Ceviche
Served in a coconut shell with summer salsa, and cassava chips
Wine Pairing: Hahn Pinot Gris

Crab Cakes
Paired with summer salsa, tomato-ginger jam, and frisée salad
Wine Pairings: Hahn SLH Chardonnay or Hahn Pinot Gris

Crab Salad with Wafer-Thin Crostini
Tossed in a honey Dijonnaise paired with frisée salad and
sweet corn ice cream
Wine Pairing: Hahn SLH Chardonnay

Jerk-Rubbed Chilean Sea bass with Tuna Tartar
Served on a polenta round with mango papaya salsa, and
avocado rose
Wine Pairing: Hahn Pinot Gris

Prawn Cocktail
Paired with a blush cocktail sauce, crudités, and lettuce chiffonade
Wine Pairing: Hahn SLH Chardonnay

Salmon Gravlax
Thinly-sliced cured salmon paired with a watercress dressing
Wine Pairing: Hahn SLH Chardonnay

Trio of Tuna
Sashimi-grade tuna tataki, smoked tuna in a cucumber shell,
and tuna nigiri with black heirloom rice
Wine Pairings: Hahn Pinot Gris or Hahn Chardonnay

Soups

Carrot and Ginger Soup
Served with micro greens and crème fraîche
Wine Pairings: Hahn Chardonnay or Hahn SLH Chardonnay

Cauliflower and Fennel Emulsion
Paired with seared scallops, balsamic vinegar pearls, and chives
Wine Pairings: Hahn Pinot Gris or Hahn Chardonnay

Frothy Lobster Bisque
Served with lobster salad, herbed panko, sweet corn
purée, and micro greens
Wine Pairing: Hahn SLH Chardonnay

Prawn Chowder
Topped with seared prawns, fresh herbs, and tortilla chips
Wine Pairings: Hahn Pinot Gris or Hahn Chardonnay

Roasted Carrot and Brie Bisque
Served with brûléed goat cheese crostini, and fresh herbs
Wine Pairings: Hahn Pinot Gris or Hahn SLH Chardonnay

Entrées

Meat

Seven Hours of Roasted Leg of Lamb
Served with green beans, braised mirepoix of vegetables,
mushroom, demi-glace, mashed potatoes, and sweet potato chips
Wine Pairing: Lucienne Doctor's Vineyard Pinot Noir
or Smith & Hook Cabernet Sauvignon

Five-Spice Duck Breast
On a potato croquette paired with orange-infused fennel, green
beans, and a sweet and spicy orange glaze
Wine Pairing: Lucienne Lone Oak Vineyard Pinot Noir

Short Rib Massaman Curry
Paired with fragrant jasmine rice and naan bread
Wine Pairing: Lucienne Smith Vineyard Pinot Noir

Sous Vide Filet Mignon
Paired with truffle pomme purée, asparagus, mushroom duxelle,
and bordelaise sauce
Wine Pairing: Smith & Hook Cabernet Sauvignon

Sous Vide Herb-Encrusted Rack of Lamb
On a polenta round paired with ratatouille, green beans,
and herb sauce
Wine Pairing: Hahn GSM

Sous Vide Pork Tenderloin
With braised cipollini onions, cauliflower emulsion, green beans,
Campari tomatoes, seared gnocchi, and pancetta crisp
Wine Pairing: Lucienne Lone Oak Vineyard Pinot Noir

Sous Vide Ribeye
On a bed of spaghetti squash with roasted cherry tomatoes, green
beans, and horseradish cream
Wine Pairing: Lucienne Smith Vineyard Pinot Noir

Seafood

Desserts

Chocolate Soufflé
Paired with crème anglaise and edible flowers
Wine Pairing: Lucienne Doctor's Vineyard Pinot Noir

Chocolate Torte Round
Served with raspberry, sweet crumble, dehydrated pineapple,
and chocolate ice cream
Wine Pairing: Lucienne Smith Vineyard Pinot Noir

Coconut Panna Cotta
Paired with fresh fruit, toasted pine nuts, mint, and edible flowers
Wine Pairing: Hahn Pinot Gris

Dark Chocolate Mousse
Stuffed with Ferrero Roche chocolate, topped with raspberry and
mint, and served under a dome of cherrywood smoke
Wine Pairings: Lucienne Smith Vineyard Pinot Noir
or Smith & Hook Cabernet Sauvignon

Frozen Bittersweet Chocolate Tart
Paired with raspberry, dehydrated pineapple, chocolate crumble,
macaroon, and bittersweet chocolate ice cream
Wine Pairing: Smith & Hook Proprietary Red Blend

Hahn GSM Poached Pear
Stuffed with a chocolate truffle and finished with crumiel crisp,
mascarpone whip, and red wine reduction
Wine Pairing: Hahn GSM

Healthy Dried Fruit Truffles
Dusted with pistachio, cocoa, and shredded coconut
Wine Pairing: Lucienne Smith Vineyard Pinot Noir

New York Cheesecake
Finished with a mirror glaze and paired with chocolate garnish
and dried and fresh fruit
Wine Pairings: Hahn SLH Chardonnay or the Hahn Pinot Noir

HOW TO USE THE BOOK

The majority of kitchens on yachts, known as galleys, have very limited space. Many of the recipes in my book were developed and executed in these tiny areas, attesting to the fact that gourmet cuisine can be created in the smallest of spaces whether in a yacht, apartment, condo, or home.

We yacht chefs and cooks battle the ocean's elements; preparing food while sailing on a 10- to 30-degree angle in large waves is a difficult task. This is why many of my recipes have been developed to include directions for advance preparation. It is optimal to always be organized and well prepared for any occasion, whether it be on a yacht or at home. Preparing your mise en place* prior to service maintains an organized and well-prepared kitchen. If you are entertaining at home, it will give you more time to mingle and entertain your guests. It will also provide the platform for a stress-free environment prior to service and plating. Knowing that I have everything well prepared in advance is the key to success in my kitchen.

Many dishes in this book are comprised of several individual recipes. Together these recipes form the different levels of flavors and textures in that particular dish. Using your creative imagination, it is possible to mix and match individual recipes to create a new signature dish of your own. An example of this is the Dark Chocolate Mousse and the Tiered Chocolate Mousse desserts that both utilize the same mousse base. The base is formed in two separate ways and finished with different garnishes to create two completely different desserts!

When preparing these recipes, always try to use fresh ingredients of the highest quality to ensure an amazing finished product. When the yacht travels to a new location, I immediately source the local farmers market. If I am to stay in the location for an extended period of time, I always develop relationships with local farmers, visiting their farms and promoting their products. By doing this, I find most farmers are willing to grow and harvest specific ingredients that I request.

You will find throughout the book that I tend to cook with European-sized portions as this is the preference for most guests. If you desire, it is possible to increase the portion sizes.

Throughout the book there are ingredients and cooking techniques that are marked with an asterisk (*). This signifies that a definition can be found in the glossary section at the back of the book. The definitions are listed in alphabetical order.

Also located at the back of the book is Back to Basics. This is a compilation of basic culinary components that I always have readily available in my kitchen or freezer. Having these ingredients on hand for everyday use can elevate even the simplest dish into a gourmet experience. Taking the time to prepare these components in advance eliminates the need to prepare them on the day of service, saving you a great deal of time.

INTRODUCTION TO THE PACOJET

I personally prepare the ice cream recipes showcased in this book using a Pacojet machine. If you have the means, I highly recommend investing in one of these useful machines.

You may also prepare the ice cream recipes using a traditional ice cream machine, or purchase ready-made from the freezer isle. Bear in mind, a homemade ice cream formed into a beautiful quenelle is truly something special, almost magical, and worth the extra effort.

I won my first Pacojet when I took First Place Chef Overall during the SCYE Concours de Chefs competition in St. Martin. It instantly became one of my favorite gourmet appliances. The Pacojet has the ability to produce exquisite savory and sweet preparations, from ice creams, sorbets, gelatos, sherbets, and mousses to farces, tartars, soups, sauces, herb concentrates, whipped cream, chopped herbs, and nuts.

The "pacotizing" process was first developed by Wilhelm Maurer in the 1980s. His patent was later sold to Pacojet in 1988 where Swiss specialists then designed the first Pacojet, an ultimate gourmet tool for commercial and home kitchens.

For frozen applications, fresh ingredients are placed into a Pacojet beaker and frozen in a freezer to -18°C/-0.4°F to -22°C/-8°F. Once frozen, the beaker is attached to the Pacojet machine. Desired portions are chosen and under high pressure, the Pacojet blade blends the ingredients, producing an ultra-smooth, delicious finished product.

INTRODUCTION
TO SOUS VIDE

Cooking In The Kitchen Sink

Have you ever stood in the kitchen wishing you did not have to check your oven roast every ten minutes, or that you could mingle with your guests just prior to service instead of slaving over the stovetop?

Sous vide eliminates these concerns and many more. This cooking technique gives you the ability to cook to the exact desired level of doneness each time and is an unbelievable feat for any kitchen. I have been utilizing the sous vide method in my galley since 2008 after purchasing *Chef Thomas Keller's* cookbook *Under Pressure,* and I could not imagine a life without this invaluable tool.

In this book, I have added a few of my favorite sous vide recipes, most of which provide the traditional cooking method as well. If you are new to the science of sous vide, I recommended becoming comfortable with the dish using the traditional method and then advancing your techniques and trying the magic of sous vide.

History and Definition of Sous Vide
Sous vide is a French term meaning "under vacuum" and was originally developed in the 1970s to cook foie gras in a vacuum-sealed bag at a low temperature in order to minimize product loss. It was later utilized in the kitchen to cook a variety of ingredients under a precise temperature and cooking time.

Essentially, sous vide is the process of cooking food in a vacuum-sealed bag to a very precise temperature using a circulated water bath. The technique uses a machine that is equipped with a thermostat and small circulation pump.

Cooking calculations for the sous vide methods are all based on the type of food, preferred doneness, and thickness of the product that you would like to cook. Today the internet holds a wealth of recipes and information guiding you to the perfect times and temperatures for a plethora of ingredients that you may desire to cook.

Since 2011, I have personally used *Jason Logsdon's* publication *Beginning Sous Vide, Low Temperature Recipes and Techniques for Getting Started at Home,* as a base for many of my cooking times and temperatures. He is also president of the *International Sous Vide Association* where my recipe *Sous Vide Crème Brûlée,* featured in this book, recently won Best Overall Dish award in their sous vide comfort foods recipe contest. This association is a collaborative community of sous vide enthusiasts who explore the technique, learn from one another, and network with like-minded individuals.

Benefits of Cooking Sous Vide
Foremost, this method enables you to prepare restaurant-quality meals even if you are a novice cook. You will also find there is no need to slave all day in front of the cooktop, giving you the ability to cook your product to an exact desired doneness. Cooking "under vacuum" allows you to infuse a variety of flavors in one small bag. You will find the natural juices and nutrients that were once lost in traditional cooking are now preserved due to the low temperature and cooking process. With sous vide there is no need to add additional fat as you do in traditional cooking; therefore, you have a lighter and healthier dish. The cooking process breaks down collagen, fat, and connective tissue, creating a deliciously tender product that is easy to digest. Sous vide also eliminates the risk of undercooking or overcooking the meal.

Safety and Sous Vide

There are a few safety concerns that need to be recognized and respected when cooking sous vide. When you vacuum seal a product, it inhibits the development of aerobic bacteria, but it will not stop bacteria that can grow in anaerobic conditions; this includes salmonella, clostridium botulinum, E. Coli 157:H7, and listeria, which can be very harmful, if not deadly, when consumed in large quantities. At certain temperatures these bacteria can double in numbers every 20 to 30 minutes.

Listed are the safe, tolerant, danger, and extreme danger zones for harmful bacteria propagation.

Temperature Zones

- 37.4°F/3°C: below this temperature food is considered in the secure or safe zone (refrigerated or frozen items)
- 39.2°F/4°C to 50°F/10°C: tolerance zone (when you allow product to come to room temperature)
- 51.8°F/11°C to 68°F/20°C: initial danger zone (minimal bacterial growth)
- 69.8°F/21°C to 122°F/49°C: extreme danger zone (maximum bacteria growth)
- 122°F/50°C to 129.2°F/54°C: additional danger zone (minimal bacterial growth)
- 131°F/55°C to 140°F/60°C: tolerance zone (medium rare to medium temperature cooking zone for many proteins)
- 140°F/60°C: above this temperature is the safe pasteurization zone and sterilization zone

There are a few golden rules when cooking sous vide: practice and respect the cooking temperatures and pasteurization times; it is not ideal to store raw fish or meat that are to be sous vided for longer than two days in the refrigerator; once the product is finished cooking, it should be served immediately or flash chilled within ten minutes of removing from the sous vide bath.

A Note on Plastics

Another issue that has been raised is cooking with plastic. There has been a fear instilled in us when it comes to the absorption of harmful properties from plastic. To ensure that the plastic you use is not harmful, purchase food-grade plastic wrap and Cryovac bags that are completely BPA-free and phthalate-free.

Cooking from Frozen

With sous vide it is possible to cook from fresh or frozen. Prior to my charter season (or at least a week prior to charter), I personally prep, portion, brine, marinate, and freeze the majority of my proteins. Being organized in the galley is the key to success amidst the frenzy of a busy charter. I then have a large quantity of pre-prepared proteins that I can toss straight into the sous vide bath prior to service. The general rule of thumb for frozen meat is to divide the fresh cooking time by two and then add that number to the fresh cooking time. For example, if you're cooking pork tenderloin, the fresh cooking time is 90 minutes. For the frozen time, you add 90 + 45 minutes, which is two hours and 15 minutes total cooking time.

I also find that when I marinate and freeze fresh red meats (not previously frozen), the process of freezing and defrosting meat that has been coated in a marinade yields a more flavorful and tender product. When freezing, ice crystals form inside the muscle fibers rupturing the cell walls, tenderizing the surface, and allowing the marinade to be absorbed. This method is especially ideal for tough cuts of meat.

The Magic of SOUS VIDE

LIFE AS A YACHT CHEF

In my personal opinion, I have the most amazing job in the world. I travel the world, manage my own kitchen with an open budget, and cater to gourmet discerning clients. These experiences have brought my level of cuisine to where it is today.

Don't get me wrong, it's not all unicorns and rainbows. This job is not for the faint of heart. In this industry we work hard, at times for months straight, without a day to ourselves. Charters can creep into 14–16-hour workdays without a break and last for days or weeks on end. I personally love the challenge and when you work with an amazing group of people who stand beside you making the best of every situation, anything is possible.

It gives me the greatest joy to sit with a group of guests at the end of the evening while they describe how amazing their day has been, and how we have made this a day they will never forget.

As yacht crew, we have the opportunity to show our guests how amazing the world is on its wonderous oceans, that there are so many wonderful and stunning views and natural ecosystems around each bay. The majority of people do not see the world from our perspective, on the sea, and to me it is the greatest gift I have ever received.

Opposite: Elizabeth on the bow of *S/Y Wonderful.*

SALADS

Deconstructed Niçoise Salad

I suggest plating the ingredients for this dish prior to searing the tuna.

Note: The potato salad, honey dijonnaise, crostinis, caper herb cream cheese, and garnishes can be prepared in advance and refrigerated prior to plating. **Note:** It is easier to acheive a thin crostini when slicing a frozen, rather than fresh, baguette.

2 pounds medley mix of baby potatoes, halved
½ cup Honey Dijonnaise Dressing (see Back to Basics page 223)
½ cup minced chives or scallions
1 tablespoon minced capers
½ frozen baguette (to make crostini)
1 tablespoon extra virgin olive oil
Salt and pepper
Caper Herb Cream Cheese (recipe follows)
½ cup black sesame seeds
2 teaspoons Penzeys Bangkok Blend* or Old Bay Seasoning*
1 teaspoon salt (2nd amount)
3 pounds sashimi-grade tuna
8 ounces mixed organic greens
8 ounces cherry tomatoes, halved
1 cup medium-dice English cucumber
2½ tablespoons drained, small capers (2nd amount)
4 hard boiled eggs, peeled and quartered
1 stalk celery, thinly sliced into ribbons* using a vegetable peeler
⅓ cup olive tapenade, preferably from Niçoise olives
2 tablespoons extra virgin olive oil (2nd amount)

Preheat oven to 375°F/190°C.

Prepare the Honey Dijonnaise Dressing.

In a large saucepan, add halved potatoes with enough cold water to cover; add salt (1½ tablespoons salt per quart of water) and bring to a boil. Reduce heat slightly and cook until tender, about 10 to 15 minutes. Drain potatoes and reserve on baking sheet to cool. When cooled, transfer potatoes to a large bowl and gently stir in Honey Dijonnaise Dressing, chives, and capers. Cover and refrigerate for service.

Thinly slice frozen baguette on the bias to create the crostini. Arrange slices (do not overlap) on a Silpat* or parchment-lined baking sheet, drizzle with olive oil, and season with salt and pepper. Bake 5 to 7 minutes, or until crisp and golden. Transfer crostinis to a baking rack, cool and reserve for service. If preparing in advance, store in an airtight container for up to 1 week.

Prepare the Caper Herb Cream Cheese. Cover and refrigerate for service.

Combine sesame seeds, seasoning, and salt on a large plate. Dredge each piece of tuna in the sesame mixture, making sure to cover all sides; reserve.

To Plate

Position a 2½-inch ring mold* in the center of a serving plate. Spoon 2 heaping tablespoons of potato salad into the mold, gently press to form a circular mound, and then carefully remove the mold. Arrange greens around the potato and garnish with tomatoes, cucumber, capers, eggs, and celery ribbons*. Form the tapenade and Caper Herb Cream Cheese into two separate quenelles* and set them close to the back of each plate. Position two crostinis, so they stand upright, in the cream cheese quenelle*. Repeat process for remaining seven plates.

Heat a large sauté pan to medium-high; when hot, add oil (2nd amount). Add tuna steaks to pan and sear 1 to 1½ minutes per side (or to preferred doneness). Remove tuna to cutting board and slice on the bias. Arrange tuna on top of potato salad and serve.

Serves 8

Caper Herb Cream Cheese

6 ounces cream cheese
2 teaspoons minced capers
2½ teaspoons minced chives
½ teaspoon salt
2 teaspoons fresh lemon juice

Place all ingredients in a bowl and stir until thoroughly combined. Cover and refrigerate for service.

Duck Confit Lyonnaise Salad

I personally use the brand Rougie canned duck confit* for this dish. At times, I will also substitute boiled 5-minute eggs for sous vide eggs.

Advanced Prep (up to 12 hours before service)

1 can duck confit* (25 ounces/750 grams)
20 fresh green beans, trimmed
4 tablespoons diced bacon
1½ tablespoons minced shallot
1 tablespoon champagne or sherry vinegar
1 teaspoon Dijon mustard
2 tablespoons vegetable oil*
4 heads frisée lettuce
4 Coral Tuiles (recipe follows)
4 large eggs, at room temperature

Preheat oven to 375°F/190°C.

Remove duck legs from can and place on baking sheet fitted with a rack. Bake in oven until duck legs are thoroughly heated through to remove as much fat as possible, about 10 minutes. Remove from oven and cool. When cooled, remove meat from the legs and discard the fat and bone. Shred the meat slightly; transfer to a plate lined with paper towel, cover and reserve.

Prepare ice bath in advance by combining ice and water in a large bowl.

In a medium saucepan, bring liberally salted water to a boil (1½ tablespoons salt per quart of water). Add beans and blanch until desired tenderness, about 3 to 4 minutes. Immediately remove from heat and transfer beans to ice bath to stop the cooking process. After 5 minutes, remove beans from ice bath, pat dry, cut into ½-inch pieces and reserve for plating.

Heat a sauté pan over medium heat. When hot, add diced bacon and cook until bacon is just crispy. Reserve 1 tablespoon bacon fat for vinaigrette preparation. Transfer bacon with a slotted spoon to a plate lined with a paper towel and reserve for plating.

For vinaigrette: In a small sauté pan, heat reserved 1 tablespoon bacon fat on medium-low heat; add minced shallots and cook until translucent, about 3 to 4 minutes. Remove pan from heat and whisk in the vinegar, mustard, and vegetable oil*; cover and reserve for service.

Remove the core from each frisée and pull into bite-size pieces. Wash greens, drain, and dry thoroughly, and reserve in refrigerator for service.

Coral Tuiles

⅔ cup water
¼ cup vegetable oil
2 tablespoons all-purpose flour
3 drops black food coloring or color of choice

In a bowl, combine all ingredients and whisk vigorously to emulsify*.

Immediately divide the mixture equally into four separate bowls. It is very important to do this while the mixture is combined, as it will separate very quickly.

Heat a dry sauté pan with a 7-inch cooking surface over medium heat. When pan is hot, whisk the batter of one bowl and pour the entire contents into the pan. Roll the pan with your wrist to ensure the batter covers the entire surface and tap lightly to flatten. Allow batter to cook and crackle until all the water evaporates, the spitting stops, and a crisp tuile remains in the oil. Using the tip of a knife, carefully remove tuile from pan and place on paper towel to absorb excess oil.

Remove the remaining oil in the pan with a paper towel. Repeat cooking steps with remaining three bowls of batter. Reserve tuiles on the counter for plating. **Note:** If preparing in advance, cool the tuiles and store in an airtight container for up to 1 day.

Service

For the eggs: Prepare ice bath in advance by combining ice and water in a large bowl.
Bring a medium saucepan of water to full boil. Using a slotted spoon, lower eggs carefully into the boiling water and cook for exactly 5 minutes. Remove the eggs with slotted spoon and transfer to ice bath for 10 seconds. Take the eggs from the bath and gently crack, peel, and remove the shells. Reserve for plating.

For the duck confit*: Reheat on the paper towel-lined plate in the microwave until warmed, about 2 to 3 minutes.

For the frisée: Place greens in a large bowl; whisk the reserved vinaigrette to re-emulsify* and toss greens with vinaigrette.

To Plate

Portion frisèe in the center of four salad bowls. Garnish the frisèe with equal portions of crispy bacon, green beans, and duck confit*. To finish: Top the salad with a soft-boiled egg and coral tuile.

Serves 4

Lobster Salad

Note: All ingredients can be prepared up to 12 hours prior to service.

Balsamic Glaze, optional garnish (see Back to Basics page 213)
Basil Oil, optional garnish (see Back to Basics page 214)
Parmesan Tuile (recipe follows)
2 quarts Court Bouillon (see Back to Basics page 219)
½ cup Honey Dijonnaise Dressing (see Back to Basics page 223)
8 uncooked lobster tails, shells intact (4 ounces each)
2 pounds mixed medley baby potatoes, halved
¼ cup minced chives or scallions
1½ teaspoons extra virgin olive oil
2 cups thinly cut, half-moon shaped, sweet onion slices
¾ cup ¼-inch dice cooked chorizo sausage
1½ cups fresh peas
2 celery stalks
8 ounces mixed organic greens
8 ounces cherry tomatoes, halved

Prepare Balsamic Glaze, Basil Oil, Parmesan Tuile, Court Bouillon, and Honey Dijonnaise Dressing.

Remove lobster tails from refrigerator and bring to room temperature. With kitchen twine*, tie 2 lobster tails together with shell sides out; the thick end of one tail facing the thin end of other. This ensures the tails do not curl when poaching. Repeat for remaining tails creating four separate bundles.

In a saucepan large enough to hold the tails, bring court bouillon to boil and reduce to simmer. Maintaining the simmer, add the tails and poach 5 to 7 minutes, or until fully cooked.

Remove tails from Court Bouillon and allow lobster to cool. Cut twine from tails and remove meat from the tails; on the underside of the tail, where the cartilage meets the shell, cut a shallow incision lengthwise down each side of the cartilage. Using gloves, carefully discard the cartilage, break open the shell and remove the meat. Reserve and refrigerate tails until service.

In a large saucepan, add halved potatoes with enough cold water to cover; add salt and bring to a boil (1½ tablespoons salt per quart of water).

Reduce heat slightly and cook until tender, about 10 to 15 minutes. Drain potatoes and reserve on baking sheet to cool. When cooled, remove potatoes to a large bowl and gently stir in Honey Dijonnaise Dressing and chives. Cover and refrigerate for service.

Heat a skillet over medium-high heat and add olive oil and onions. Cook onions, stirring frequently until caramelized, about 10 to 12 minutes. Add chorizo and peas and sauté an additional 2 minutes. Allow mixture to cool and just before service, gently combine with reserved potatoes.

Trim celery stalks and thinly slice lengthwise with a vegetable peeler. Reserve strips in a bowl of ice water to create a curled effect for the garnish.

To Plate

Place a portion of potato salad in the center of each serving plate and arrange mixed greens decoratively around the salad. Top the potato salad with a lobster tail and garnish with cherry tomatoes, celery strips, a Parmesan Tuile, Balsamic Glaze, and Basil Oil.

Serves 8

Parmesan Tuiles

⅓ cup grated Parmesan-Reggiano cheese*

Preheat oven to 350°F/177°C.

On a Silpat* or parchment-lined baking sheet, divide the grated cheese into 8 portions. Using your fingertips, spread the portions of cheese evenly into 2-inch rounds.

Bake tuiles, watching carefully that they do not burn, until they are golden brown, about 8 to 10 minutes. Remove tuiles from the oven and rest 1 minute. Carefully transfer the tuiles to a paper towel. Use immediately or cool and store in an airtight container for up to 24 hours.

Note: It is important to use fresh and moist Parmesan-Reggiano cheese* to create a light and airy product.

Seared Shrimp Salad

This salad is always a guest favorite. I love to slice the shrimps in half lengthwise, so they curl as they cook, adding an additional visual appeal. It is possible to substitute the 16/20 count shrimp with any size, just alter the cooking time to ensure your shrimp is thoroughly cooked.

Note: Quinoa, sliced shrimp (prior to cooking), feta cheese, and vegetables can be prepared in advance and reserved in the refrigerator for plating.

6 ounces mixed organic salad greens
27 cherry tomatoes
1 English cucumber, trimmed and peeled
1 celery stalk
6 sprigs cilantro
3½ ounces feta cheese
2 pounds shrimp, peeled, deveined, tails removed (16/20 count)
1 teaspoon sea salt
1 teaspoon white pepper
½ teaspoon smoked paprika
1 tablespoon extra virgin olive oil
1 clove garlic, minced
½ cup dry white wine, Hahn Pinot Gris
½ cup heavy cream (36% M.F.)
2½ cups cooked Quinoa Pilaf (recipe follows)
½ cup micro greens, alfalfa, or broccoli sprouts

Rinse salad greens, slice cherry tomatoes in half, and dice cucumber into ¼-inch cubes. Slice celery on the bias into 12 long, thin wedges; cover and refrigerate vegetables for service.

Remove leaves from cilantro sprigs and mince; discard stalks. In a small bowl, crumble feta cheese and add minced cilantro. Toss to combine, cover and refrigerate herbed feta for service.

Slice shrimp in half lengthwise and season with salt, white pepper, and smoked paprika.

Heat a sauté pan over medium heat. When hot, add olive oil and shrimp; sauté until shrimp begin to turn pink and curl, about 2 to 3 minutes. Stir in garlic and cook 1 minute longer. Add wine to sauté pan and reduce by half, about 2 to 3 minutes. Add the cream, bring to simmer and cook 1 minute. (The sauce will become your warm vinaigrette.)

To Plate

Divide the Quinoa Pilaf into the base of six serving dishes. With a spoon, create a well in the pilaf to provide a base for the greens. Top pilaf with salad greens and arrange the tomatoes and cucumber around the pilaf. Place seared shrimp on top of greens and drizzle with warm vinaigrette. Finish with the herbed feta and sprouts. Arrange celery garnish decoratively on the side of salad.

Quinoa Pilaf

½ cup white quinoa
½ cup black or red quinoa
2 cups water
1 teaspoon dried oregano
1 teaspoon dried basil
½ teaspoon celery salt
Salt and pepper

In a 3-quart saucepan, combine quinoa, water, and seasonings; stir to combine. Bring to a boil, reduce to a low boil, cover and cook 20 minutes or until quinoa becomes translucent and the germ shows a visible spiral on the exterior of the grains.

Remove from heat and let stand, covered, for 5 minutes or until all stock is absorbed. Fluff with a fork, season with salt and pepper if desired, and reserve.

Yields 2 ½ cups pilaf

Serves 6

Sous Vide Grilled Skirt Steak Salad

Sous Vide Grilled Skirt Steak Salad

Two of my favorite proteins to sous vide are skirt and flank steaks. With the process of sous vide, you have the ability to turn a tough cut of meat into something that is tender, full of flavor, and melt-in-your-mouth delicious. At the beginning of my charter season, I purchase a large quantity of both flank and skirt steaks for batch processing. I will sous vide them and once complete, flash chill and freeze the meat to ensure I have this beautiful steak on hand throughout the season. To use, simply defrost, sear, and serve.

Advanced Prep (all ingredients up to 12 hours before service, and the sous vide steak can be prepared and frozen up to 2 to 3 months in advance)

2 outside skirt or flank steaks, 5 to 6 ounces each
1 teaspoon brown sugar
2 teaspoons Penzeys Mitchell Street Seasoning* or Montreal Steak Seasoning*
1¾ teaspoons Worcestershire sauce*
3 tablespoons extra virgin olive oil
48 Oven-Dried Cherry Tomatoes (see Back to Basics page 226)
Grilled Vegetables (see Back to Basics page 222)
Porcini Couscous (recipe follows)
Blue Cheese Dressing (recipe follows)
8 ounces mixed organic greens
12 basil sprigs

With a sharp knife, trim the excess fat and sinew* from the steaks. Pierce the meat all over with a fork to tenderize.

Rub the steaks with sugar and seasoning and place in a Ziploc bag or container. Combine the Worcestershire sauce* and olive oil; pour mixture over meat and liberally rub it in. Seal the bag or cover the container and refrigerate for at least 4 hours and up to 2 days. If marinating for longer than 4 hours, turn at least 4 to 5 times during the marinating process.

Prepare the cherry tomatoes, grilled vegetables, couscous, and dressing. Rinse the mixed greens and basil leaves, pat dry, and reserve in refrigerator for plating.

For the *sous vide cooking method*, follow the directions below after the steak has marinated in the refrigerator.
For the *traditional cooking method*, omit this step.

SOUS VIDE METHOD
Preheat sous vide bath to 131°F/55°C or preferred internal temperature.
Using a Cryovac* machine and commercial-grade vacuum-seal

bag, seal the steaks following machine directions.
Ensure the steaks lie flat inside the bag and do not overlap. Each steak will now have maximum surface area while cooking in the water bath.

Once the sous vide bath has reached the exact temperature (no less), completely submerge the sealed steaks into the bath. Allow to sous vide for 24 to 48 hours.

Service

If using the *traditional cooking method*, remove the steak from the refrigerator 1 to 1½ hours before grilling to allow to come to room temperature.

Preheat grill to medium-high, 400°F/205°C to 450°F/235°C.

Make sure the grill is clean and piping hot. The grill is used for the *traditional cooking method* and to finish the sous vide steak.

For the *sous vide steak*: Once the cooking process is complete, remove vacuum bag from the water bath and remove the steak from the bag. Transfer the steak to a plate and pat dry; discard the bag and its contents. Sear the steaks on the grill, 1½ to 2 minutes per side and then remove to a cutting board to rest while you plate the dish.

Note: As a *sous vide steak* is already cooked, it is grilled only to give additional color, flavor, and texture. It is important to have a very hot grill that will give the steak a "charred" effect.

For the *traditional steak*: once the steak has come to room temperature, sear the steak on the grill until an optimal internal temperature has been achieved, depending on preferred doneness. Remove steak to a cutting board to rest while you plate the dish.

To Plate

I prefer to use rectangular serving plates for the presentation of this dish.

Thinly slice the steak. Place a small mound of couscous onto each plate, create a bed of lettuce on the couscous, and decoratively garnish the lettuce with the steak, grilled vegetables, oven-dried cherry tomatoes, and basil leaves. Serve the blue cheese dressing in a small ramekin or individual 1- to 2-ounce cream pitchers.

Serves 6

Porcini Couscous

2 teaspoons extra virgin olive oil
½ pound porcini mushrooms or mushroom variety of choice, finely chopped
3 tablespoons minced shallots
¼ teaspoon salt
¼ teaspoon freshly ground black pepper
2 tablespoons unsalted butter
1 tablespoon fresh thyme leaves, or ½ teaspoon dried thyme
1¼ cups water or chicken or vegetable broth
1 cup couscous

Heat a large sauté pan over medium heat. When pan is hot, add the olive oil, mushrooms, shallots, and salt and pepper; cook, stirring frequently, until the mushrooms appear dry and are beginning to brown, about 5 to 6 minutes. Stir in the butter and thyme and remove from heat.

In a medium-sized heavy-bottomed saucepan, bring water or broth to a boil over medium-high heat. Remove saucepan from heat, stir in the couscous, cover and rest 5 minutes. Remove the cover, fluff the couscous with a fork and transfer to a medium bowl. Stir in the cooked mushroom mixture and reserve for service.

Blue Cheese Dressing

¼ cup mayonnaise (see Back to Basics page 224)
⅓ cup sour cream
1 tablespoon fresh lemon juice
¼ teaspoon Worcestershire sauce*
¼ teaspoon salt
¼ teaspoon pepper
3 tablespoons half-and-half (10% M.F.)
⅓ cup crumbled blue cheese

In a medium bowl, whisk together all ingredients except the blue cheese.

Gently stir in the blue cheese, cover and refrigerate for service. *If you desire a thinner consistency, gently whisk in additional half and half.

Below: Batch processing skirt steaks with a commericial sous vide machine.

S/Y Wonderful anchored in Mayreau island,
Saint Vincent and the Grenadines

S/Y WONDERFUL LIVING THE DREAM

In 2006, three years after I entered the yachting industry, I finally found a yacht and crew where I felt at home. This is where I met Warren East, my future husband and partner in life and love. During our time onboard, we sailed over 150,000 miles, experiencing diverse cultures, tasting and learning about their ethnic cuisines along the way. *Wonderful,* an amazing yacht, could take on almost all prevailing sea conditions, elegantly gliding across the surface of the water, enabling her captain and crew to always feel safe.

My six years on board were a dream; sailing to the far reaches of the Atlantic Ocean and the Caribbean, Mediterranean, and Red Seas. After five trans-Atlantic crossings, people would always ask, "Why would you want to sail across an ocean, weeks at sea without a glimpse of land in sight?"

Above, left: *S/Y Wonderful* in the Corinth Canal; right: filleting mahi mahi mid-Atlantic.

This is a very easy answer for anyone who has ever experienced the true magic the ocean holds. It is an exhilarating feeling to sail off into a beautiful sunset surrounded by fresh air and colors that blend into the sky like a watercolor painting that is only for your eyes to behold. Whales and dolphins dance alongside over the deep abyss, as ocean birds soar overhead. At night the ocean can be glassy calm with the stars reflecting in the shimmering water, causing it to appear as though you are floating in space, only to be broken by a stream of glowing phosphorescence, as dolphins race to the bow resembling shooting stars in space.

These are just a few of the countless memories from our journeys across the vast oceans.

S/Y Wonderful will always have a very special place in my heart. Her name, a testament to life on a yacht.

Above, left: *S/Y Wonderful* anchored off Palm Island, Saint Vincent and the Grenadines; right: hoisting the sails.

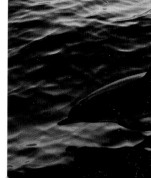

Above: sunset in the Aeolian Islands. Middle: dolphin in the Atlantic Ocean.
Opposite, top: sunrise in the middle of the Atlantic Ocean.
Opposite, middle: Warren in Saint Lucia. Opposite, right: tree on the beach, Saint John, USVI.

APPETIZERS

Caprese Salad

My husband and I spent two summers working on a yacht that was based in Port Santo Stefano, Italy. I am in love with the Mediterranean, especially with Italian summers; the food, culture, and energy of life is simply breathtaking. Here is where I fell in love with the caprese salad, a dish that I adore.

This classic Italian recipe is light, fresh, and easy to prepare. For optimum flavor, use the sweet and juicy heirloom tomatoes readily available in summer and fall. Heirloom tomatoes are a step back in times to the tomato of yesteryear and are grown using open-pollinated seeds that have been passed down from generation to generation with no genetic alteration. The incomparable flavor, aroma, variety of color, and tenderness of organically grown heirloom tomatoes bears no resemblance to the everyday generic fruit. You can substitute regular store bought tomatoes, which are available year round, but will sacrifice much of the flavor.

Note: In this recipe I use Basil Oil that requires 24 hours advance preparation. If time is an issue, substitute extra virgin olive oil or store-purchased pesto. Opposite photo (page 54): an alternate plating to the plating that is described below.

Basil Oil or Pesto Alla Genovese (see Back to Basics page 214, 226)
Balsamic Glaze (see Back to Basics page 213)
Balsamic Vinegar Pearls (see Back to Basics page 213)
½ pound heirloom tomatoes, use a variety of shapes, colors, and sizes
4 to 6 ounces buffalo mozzarella*, bocconcini, or fresh mozzarella cheese
½ teaspoon salt
½ teaspoon pepper
8 to 12 whole, large basil leaves
¼ cup thinly sliced red onion
4 to 6 basil sprigs

Prepare the Basil Oil or Pesto Alla Genovese, Balsamic Glaze, and Balsamic Vinegar Pearls.

Slice the tomatoes into rounds or halves ¼-inch thick or less. If you would like to cut the tomatoes in advance, place the slices on a plate lined with a paper towel to absorb excess moisture; cover with plastic wrap and reserve in refrigerator.

Cut each mozzarella ball into 8 round slices ¼-inch thick or less. If you would like to cut the cheese in advance, place the slices on a plate lined with a paper towel to absorb excess moisture; cover with plastic wrap and reserve in refrigerator.

To Plate

Lightly season tomatoes with salt and pepper. Fan two or three slices of tomato on each plate as a base. Top with a whole basil leaf, a slice of mozzarella, second slice of tomato, basil leaf, second mozzarella slice, and top with thinly sliced red onion. Garnish with basil sprigs and Balsamic Vinegar Pearls. To finish: drizzle with Basil Oil or Pesto Alla Genovese and Balsamic Glaze.

Serves 4 to 6

Goat Cheese Soufflé

I love the magic of the soufflé. To sit in front of the oven and literally watch as they rise gives me the same excitement I felt as a child opening gifts on Christmas morning.

The soufflé has always been one of my favorite savory dishes and once you have the technique in place, you are able to create sweet and savory soufflés with any flavor.

Note: For this dish, it is possible to prepare the base 4 to 6 hours in advance. Reserve the base on the counter at room temperature until you are ready for service.

Balsamic Glaze (see Back to Basics page 213)
Finger Crostini (recipe follows)
1½ cups Béchamel (see Back to Basics page 215)
6 large eggs, separated and reserved in 2 separate bowls
2 teaspoons Dijon mustard
¼ cup grated Parmigiano-Reggiano cheese
½ cup crumbled goat cheese
¾ teaspoon salt
White pepper
Fresh herbs, for garnish

Prepare the Balsamic Glaze and Finger Crostini.

Preheat oven to 400°F/205°C.

In a small saucepan, heat the prepared béchamel until the mixture barely reaches a simmer. Remove from heat and whisk in egg yolks, mustard, and Parmigiano-Reggiano cheese. Cool mixture slightly; fold in goat cheese and season with salt and pepper to taste.

In a bowl or mixer, whip egg whites until soft peaks form. Gently fold whites into béchamel mixture.

Lightly spray eight ramekins (½-cup size) with vegetable oil*. Ladle mixture into each ramekin up to the filling line that is found below the rim. Bake, resisting any temptation to open oven door, until beautifully puffed and golden brown, about 13 to 15 minutes. Serve immediately.

To Plate

Note: It is best to prepare the plates with crostini, herbs, and balsamic garnish before removing soufflés from oven. When soufflés are ready, rapidly plate and serve.

Garnish each plate with Balsamic Glaze, 4 Finger Crostinis, and herbs. Optional, fold a cocktail napkin and place under the ramekin to ensure that the dish will not slide.

Serves 8

Finger Crostini

8 slices white or whole wheat sandwich bread
1 tablespoon extra virgin olive oil
Salt and pepper

Preheat oven to 400°F/205°C.

Remove crusts from bread slices. Cut each slice into 4 equal crostini fingers, brush with olive oil and season with salt and pepper. Arrange crostini on a baking sheet and bake until golden brown, about 8 to 10 minutes. Remove from oven and cool on baking rack.

Italian Sushi

When I was working at the Trattoria di Umberto in Whistler, British Columbia, Canada, I would utilize antipasto from the previous night's service to create these delectable tasty treats. You can substitute the zucchini with eggplant and stuff the sushi with any form of vegetable, meat, or cheese.

Italian Sushi makes a great snack, hors d'oeuvre, or appetizer. You can even pair it with a salad to create a main course.

Note: Italian sushi rolls and garnishes can be prepared in advance; store in the refrigerator prior to plating.

Balsamic Glaze (see Back to Basics page 213)
3 to 4 medium zucchini
1 red bell pepper
10 asparagus spears
¼ cup balsamic vinegar
¼ teaspoon salt
¼ teaspoon pepper
¾ cup extra virgin olive oil
¼ teaspoon Dijon mustard
1 garlic clove, minced
½ teaspoon liquid honey
Herb Cream Cheese (recipe follows)
1 English cucumber
12 cherry tomatoes, thinly sliced
6 ounces thinly-sliced prosciutto
20 basil leaves (2-inch lengths)
1½ cups mixed salad greens
12 basil sprigs

Prepare Balsamic Glaze.

Preheat grill to medium-high, 400°F/205°C to 450°F/235°C.

Trim ends of zucchini and then slice lengthwise into ¼-inch thick slices. This should yield about 20 slices. Cut bell pepper in half lengthwise and remove seeds, membrane, and stem. Cut pepper halves in ½-inch strips.

Remove the fibrous ends from the asparagus.

In a bowl, combine vinegar, salt and pepper; add olive oil in a slow steady stream, whisking constantly until emulsified. Toss the zucchini, bell pepper, and asparagus in some of the vinaigrette, just to coat. Place the remaining vinaigrette in a small bowl and add the Dijon mustard, garlic, and honey; whisk to re-emulsify* and reserve.

Arrange zucchini slices on the preheated grill; grill zucchini, turning once, until marked and cooked through, about 6 minutes. Grill pepper and asparagus, turning as needed, until cooked through, about 4 to 6 minutes depending on vegetable thickness. As vegetables finish cooking, remove from grill and allow to cool.

Cut the asparagus and pepper strips into 2-inch lengths when cooled.

Prepare the Herb Cream Cheese.

Halve the cucumber lengthwise and remove seeds. Using a vegetable peeler, thinly slice cucumber lengthwise to make 60 thin slices. Roll each slice into a round ribbon for garnish.

To assemble: cut prosciutto slices to fit the grilled zucchini slices and place a piece the prosciutto on top of each zucchini slice. Spoon 1½ teaspoons Herb Cream Cheese on one end of the prosciutto and top with a basil leaf, one piece of asparagus, and red pepper; roll to form a zucchini roll that resembles sushi. Repeat the procedure, making 18 to 20 rolls in total. Lightly toss mixed greens with reserved vinaigrette.

To Plate

Place three Italian sushi rolls in the center of each plate and garnish with mixed greens, cucumber ribbon rounds, cherry tomatoes, basil sprigs, and Balsamic Glaze.

Serves 6

Herb Cream Cheese

Use this versatile cheese spread to stuff miniature sweet bell peppers or spread on crackers and crostini.

8 ounces cream cheese, room temperature
1 garlic clove, minced
¼ teaspoon fresh oregano or pinch of dried
½ teaspoon fresh basil or ⅛ teaspoon dried
½ teaspoon fresh rosemary, chopped, or ⅛ teaspoon dried and crushed
⅛ teaspoon salt

In a bowl, blend all ingredients until smooth and creamy. Cover and refrigerate.

Yields 1 cup

Seared Hellim Bruschetta

This dish uses the popular and delicious Turkish hellim cheese; also known as halloumi in Greece. In this recipe the mild, salty cheese is complemented with the crunch of fresh toasted bread and a cool, savory tomato bruschetta, making it an ideal snack for any time of the day.

The high melting point of hellim cheese allows it to become golden brown and retain its shape even at high temperatures. Serve as an appetizer, hors d'oeuvre, or pair with a salad for lunch.

Note: The tomato mixture, crostinis, and garnishes can be prepared in advance.

½ teaspoon Balsamic Glaze (see Back to Basics page 213)
1¼ cups seeded, ¼-inch diced vine-ripened tomatoes
2 tablespoons minced chives
¼ teaspoon minced garlic
¼ teaspoon granulated sugar
½ teaspoon extra virgin olive oil
Salt and pepper
8 slices white or whole wheat sandwich bread, crusts removed
1 tablespoon extra virgin olive oil (2nd amount)
1 pound hellim cheese
Fresh basil or micro herbs

Prepare Balsamic Glaze in advance.

Preheat oven to 400°F/205°C.

In a bowl, add tomatoes, chives, garlic, sugar, and oil; stir to combine. Adjust seasoning with salt and pepper to taste. Refrigerate until service, allowing flavors to blend.

Halve each slice of bread to make 16 rectangle-shaped crostinis. Brush each crostini with olive oil and place on parchment or Silpat*-lined baking sheet and bake until golden brown, about 8 to 10 minutes.

Slice cheese into 16 rectangular ¼-inch thick slices. Heat a large non-stick sauté pan over medium-high heat and sear cheese on each side until golden, about 1½ to 2 minutes per side.

To Plate

Place 2 crostini on each plate; top with seared hellim and the tomato mixture. Garnish with fresh basil or micro greens and a drizzle of Balsamic Glaze.

Serves 8

Norman's Cay, Exuma Islands, Bahamas

Duck Confit

W hile studying the ethnic cuisine of the southern coast of Turkey, I was fortunate enough to gain immense knowledge from a lady who had six generations of traditional Turkish gastronomy in her family, and she did not speak a word of English!

One of the many dishes that I learned was this basic lentil rissole, traditionally served wrapped in crisp lettuce leaves.

It became one of my favorite Turkish delights, and I have depicted it here with a modern twist.

Note: There will be about 2 cups of the lentil rissole mixture left over. Freeze for future use or mold remaining mixture into vegetable burgers. Separate the burgers with parchment paper and use within 3 to 4 days or freeze. The burgers are very versatile and can be served cold, heated, or sautéed.

Advanced Prep (up to 12 hours before service)

Hahn GSM Onion Chutney (see Back to Basics page 223)
Citrus Gremolata (recipe follows)
1 can duck confit* (25 ounces/750 grams)
1 cup split red lentils*
2½ cups water, vegetable broth, or chicken broth
1 cup finely ground bulgur wheat*
2 tablespoons extra virgin olive oil
⅓ cup finely diced white onion
2 garlic cloves, minced
2 tablespoons tomato paste
¼ cup chopped fresh parsley
1 tablespoon chopped cilantro
1 teaspoon cumin
1 teaspoon smoked Spanish paprika
1 teaspoon salt
¼ teaspoon pepper
2 tablespoons sesame or vegetable oil*
1⅓ cups chiffonade* butter lettuce
6 cilantro sprigs

Prepare Hahn GSM Onion Chutney and Citrus Gremolata.

Preheat oven to 375°F/190°C.

Remove duck legs from can and place on baking sheet fitted with a rack. Bake in oven until duck legs are thoroughly heated to remove as much fat as possible, about 10 minutes. Remove from oven and cool. When cooled, remove meat from the legs and discard the fat and bone. Shred the meat slightly, cover and reserve.

Rinse the lentils in a strainer under cold running water. In a heavy-bottomed saucepan, add lentils and water or broth. Bring to boil, reduce to simmer, and cook, stirring occasionally, until tender, about 25 minutes.
If necessary, replenish the lentils with a minimal amount of water during the cooking process. Once tender, remove from heat and stir in bulgur wheat*. Cover and set aside to steam for 10 to 15 minutes.

While lentils are steaming, heat a sauté pan over medium heat; add olive oil, onion, and garlic and sauté until translucent, about 3 to 4 minutes. Stir in tomato paste and sauté 1 minute. Remove pan from heat and stir in parsley, cilantro, cumin, smoked Spanish paprika, and salt and pepper.

After the lentil mixture has finished steaming, transfer to a bowl and cool slightly. Fold in onion mixture and knead well with your hands. Shape the lentils into six ⅛- to ¼-cup sized patties to suit desired serving size; cover and reserve for service.

Lentil mixture yields 3½ cups.

Service

Bring a sauté pan to medium heat, add oil and sear rissoles until browned, about 2 to 3 minutes per side.

To plate

One at a time, rub each rim of six individual flared cocktail glasses (martini glasses) with a damp paper towel. Run the rim of the glass through the Citrus Gremolata so that it adheres.

Portion the lettuce chiffonade* into the bottom of each glass, top with a lentil rissole, and place 1 tablespoon chutney at its side. Top the rissole with 2 ounces of duck. Finish with a sprig of cilantro to garnish.

Serves 6

Citrus Gremolata

3 lemons
3 limes
1 tablespoon finely chopped parsley
½ teaspoon salt

Using a fine microplane* zester, zest the lemons and limes. Combine all ingredients onto a flat plate; cover and reserve for service.

Sous Vide Beef Carpaccio

Carpaccio is a delicious way to savor the genuine taste of a high-grade filet. I prefer to use USDA Black Angus Prime, Wagyu, or Kobe beef as not all tenderloins in the marketplace are equal in flavor and tenderness

I like to sous vide the steak, as this allows the flavors to permeate to the center of the filet.
Sous vide tenderizes the meat, breaking down the collagen, fat, and connective tissue to create a deliciously tender product that is easy to digest.

Advanced Prep (12 hours before service) **Note:** Sous vide filet can be prepared and frozen up to 2 to 3 months in advance.

Beef Carpaccio

1 teaspoon finely ground black pepper
½ teaspoon salt
12 ounce trimmed, whole beef tenderloin, preferably 2-inch width
1 teaspoon extra virgin olive oil
Fragrance Vegetables (recipe follows)
Honey Dijonnaise (see Back to Basics page 223)
1 small head frisée lettuce
1 teaspoon fresh lemon juice
1 tablespoon extra virgin olive oil
16 pieces shaved Parmigiano-Reggiano cheese

Evenly cover a small plate with the pepper and salt. Roll the tenderloin into the seasoning to completely encrust.

Place two pieces of plastic wrap, overlapping one another and laying flat on the counter top, to make an 18 x 18-inch square.

Place tenderloin in the center of the plastic wrap and drizzle with olive oil. Take the bottom seam of the plastic wrap and fold it over the top of the tenderloin, pull it towards you and completely cover the meat. Roll the tenderloin in the plastic wrap away from you; pinch and close the open ends of the plastic wrap and continue to pinch and roll upwards until the tenderloin is completely sealed and resembles a sausage in its casing. Tie the ends in a knot to secure. This allows the tenderloin to retain its perfect cylindrical shape for freezing and/or cooking with the *sous vide method*.

Prepare the Fragrance Vegetables and Honey Dijonnaise.

For traditional carpaccio, omit the *sous vide method* below. Place the tenderloin in the freezer for 10 to 12 hours or until frozen solid.

For the *sous vide cooking method*, follow method below.

SOUS VIDE METHOD
Preheat sous vide bath to 131°F/55°C.

Using a Cryovac* machine and commercial-grade vacuum-seal bag, seal the tenderloin following machine directions. When the sous vide has come to the correct temperature (no less), completely submerge the sealed tenderloin into the sous vide bath and cook for 2 hours.

In a large bowl, prepare ice bath with ice and water. Once the sous vide cooking is complete, remove vacuum bag to the ice bath and completely submerge for 10 to 12 minutes. Remove from ice bath, pat dry and place in freezer for 10 to 12 hours or until frozen solid. Rinse frisée, pat dry, and refrigerate for plating.

Service

Remove the beef from the freezer and thinly slice using a meat slicer, mandolin*, or sharp knife.
After cutting each slice, immediately plate 15-18 slices per plate overlapping in a perfect circle on each of 6 serving plates.

Add lemon juice to a bowl, whisking vigorously. Slowly add the oil and beat until emulsified. Toss frisée with the prepared lemon oil.

To Plate

Evenly distribute the Fragrance Vegetables on top of the carpaccio and drizzle with Honey Dijonnaise. To finish: garnish with the cheese and dressed frisée.

Serves 4

Fragrance Vegetables

1 tablespoon ⅛-inch diced carrot
1 tablespoon ⅛-inch diced red pepper
1 tablespoon ⅛-inch diced red onion
1 tablespoon ⅛-inch diced celery
5 teaspoons water
Salt and pepper

Heat a small skillet over medium heat. Using a dry pan, sauté the vegetables, stirring frequently until fragrant, about 2 minutes. Add 1 teaspoon of water every 2 minutes and continue cooking until vegetables are al dente*, about 6 to 8 minutes. Remove from pan, season with salt and pepper, and allow to cool.

Sous Vide Foie Gras

I am a lover of foie gras, and although this recipe takes time to prepare, it is well worth the effort. It can be transformed into a canapé, appetizer, lunch, or entrée and served seared, chilled, or atop a bianca pizza, which happens to be one of my husband's favorite treats.

To utilize the torchon on top of a bianca pizza, simply bake a pizza base with a mild white cheese; remove from oven and top with caramelized onions and slices of foie gras. To finish, brûleé the foie gras with a kitchen torch, slice and serve. It is truly amazing!

Note: This recipe will make an extra torchon of foie gras, as I have created a recipe to suit the purchase of a whole lobe. For leftovers, wrap foie gras in plastic wrap, Cryovac using a commercial-grade vacuum-seal bag, and freeze for later use.

Advanced Prep (up to 12 hours before service.) **Note:** Sous vide foie gras can be prepared and frozen up to 2 to 3 months in advance.

Below: Foie Gras Pizza

Foie Gras Torchon*

1 tablespoon Spice Mixture (recipe follows)
⅝ teaspoon granulated sugar
¼ teaspoon pink curing salt* (use regular salt if curing salt is not available)
1 tablespoon salt
1 whole, fresh foie gras*, Grade A, 1.75 to 2-pound size, preferably Hudson valley
3 teaspoons cognac, divided
Hahn Red Wine Reduction (recipe follows)

Prepare the Spice Mixture.

Make "curing salt mixture": in a small bowl, thoroughly combine 1 tablespoon of the Spice Mixture, sugar, pink curing salt*, and salt. **Note:** The "curing salt mixture" makes more than is necessary for the recipe, save excess for later use.

Fill a large bowl ⅔ full of cool water, add the sealed foie gras* to the water and bring slowly to room temperature, about 35 to 40 minutes. This will allow the lobe to become soft and pliable, making it easier to remove the veins.

Take the foie gras* from the water; remove the sealed packaging and pat dry. Transfer to a cutting board and split the foie gras* into two separate even pieces or lobes. Using a palette knife and tweezers, remove and discard the veins from each lobe.

Bear in mind that the lobes will be reconstructed for each torchon*, so it is fine if the lobes break apart and lose their shape.

Lay two separate overlapping triple-layers of 18 x 18-inch plastic wrap on the counter. Place one foie gras* section on each plastic wrap. Carefully butterfly each lobe using your fingertips into a 9 x 6-inch rectangle of even thickness.

Add 1 teaspoon of the curing salt mixture to a fine sieve and dust evenly over the surface of one lobe. Sprinkle the lobe with 1½ teaspoons cognac. Repeat process for second lobe.

Move the lobe, with plastic underneath, onto a bamboo sushi-rolling mat, adjusting the plastic so that the bottom edge of the lobe is flush with the bottom of the mat.

Carefully roll the lobe away from you using the mat to keep it nice and tight to form a perfect cylinder similar to a sushi roll. Roll and tighten until a perfect torchon* is formed, ensuring that the plastic wrap has not become stuck inside the cylinder. Repeat for remaining lobe.

Prepare Hahn Red Wine Reduction.

For cooking with the *sous vide cooking method*, follow the directions below.
For *traditional cooking method*, omit this step.

SOUS VIDE METHOD
Preheat sous vide bath to 104°F/40°C.

Set the bamboo sushi mat aside and roll the foie gras* in the plastic wrap away from you to create a sausage-like casing. Pinch close the open ends of the plastic wrap and continue to pinch and roll upwards until the lobe is completely sealed and resembles a sausage in its casing. This allows the foie gras* to retain its perfect cylindrical shape while cooking in the sous vide bath. Tie both ends of the plastic wrap in a knot to secure and refrigerate. Repeat for second lobe.

Using a Cryovac* machine and commercial-grade vacuum-seal bags, seal the foie gras* following machine directions. Once the sous vide bath has come to the correct temperature (no less), completely submerge the sealed lobes into the bath. Allow to sous vide for 30 minutes.

While the torchons* are sous-viding prepare ice bath by combining ice and water in a large bowl. Once the cooking process is complete, remove vacuum bags from sous vide bath and completely submerge them into the ice water bath for 15 to 20 minutes. Remove bags from ice bath, pat dry, and refrigerate for 24 to 48 hours prior to plating.

TRADITIONAL COOKING METHOD
Lay two quadruple layers of cheesecloth*, 16 x 24-inches long, on the counter.

Transfer the foie gras* from the plastic wrap onto the cheesecloth* and discard plastic. Position and center the lobe 4 inches from the bottom of the cloth. Carefully roll the lobe away from you into the cheesecloth* to create a sausage-like casing, pulling the lobe back as you roll to tighten.

Pinch the open ends of the cheesecloth* and continue to pinch and roll upwards until the lobe starts to leak out around the edges of the cloth and creates a perfect cylinder. Twist the ends of the cheesecloth* and secure tightly with kitchen twine*. Repeat for the second foie gras*. Place both lobes in the refrigerator, preferably hanging, for 24 to 48 hours.

In a large stockpot, bring a large quantity of water to just below simmer, 160°F/71°C.

Prepare ice bath by combining ice and water in a large bowl. Poach the torchons* in the hot water for 2 minutes, ensuring that they are completely submerged. Immediately transfer to the ice bath and chill 10 minutes. Remove from ice bath, thoroughly pat dry and refrigerate 24 to 48 hours prior to plating.

Spice Mixture

½ tablespoon ground Chinese five spice
½ teaspoon powdered ginger
½ teaspoon ground black pepper
¼ teaspoon ground cinnamon
1 vanilla bean, seeds removed

In a small bowl, combine all ingredients until thoroughly mixed.

Hahn Red Wine Reduction

1 bottle, 750 ml, full bodied red wine, Hahn Pinot Noir or GSM
¼ cup granulated sugar

Bring wine to a simmer and reduce until 1 cup remains, about 50 minutes. Add sugar and continue to simmer, stirring constantly, until sugar has completely dissolved. Lower temperature to low simmer and continue to cook until desired consistency is achieved, about 20 minutes.

Note: Bear in mind that the mixture will thicken as it cools.

Garnish

Hahn GSM Onion Chutney (see Back to Basics page 223)
½ cup arugula
9 slices brioche bread

Prepare the Hahn Red Onion Chutney. Rinse, pat dry, and refrigerate arugula for plating.

Remove the crusts from the brioche slices, portion into 36 triangles and reserve for service.

Service

Heat oven broiler to high. Place toast points on a Silpat* or parchment-lined baking sheet. Toast under the broiler, turning the toast points halfway through to brown both sides, about 2-3 minutes. Keep an eye on the bread as it can toast very quickly and potentially burn. Reserve for plating.

Fill a heavy-bottomed tall glass with hot water and insert an 8-inch utility knife to warm. Remove one torchon* from the refrigerator. Discard the plastic wrap or cheesecloth* and place on a cutting board. Remove the knife from the glass, pat dry, and slice the torchon* into twelve ½-inch thick slices for service.

If there is foie gras* left over, wrap tightly in plastic wrap. Using a Cryovac* machine and commercial-grade vacuum-seal bag, seal the foie gras following machine directions and freeze for later use. At this time you can also freeze the second torchon* that was prepared.

To Plate

Divide the arugula between six serving plates to create a small "bed" for the torchon* and place 2 slices on each arugula bed. Garnish each plate with Hahn GSM Onion Chutney and Hahn Red Wine Reduction. Serve with the toasted brioche points.

Note: I like to fill eight individual 1- to 2-ounce cream pitchers with the red wine reduction.

Serves 6

Pusser's Marina Cay, British Virgin Islands
Before Hurricane Irma

Summer Salsa

¼ cup ⅛-inch diced red pepper
¼ cup ⅛-inch diced mango
¼ cup ⅛-inch diced cucumber
Pinch of cumin
Salt and pepper

In a small bowl, combine red pepper, mango, cucumber, and cumin. Season to taste with salt and pepper.

Yields ¾ cup

Coconut Mahi Mahi Ceviche

Mahi mahi*, also known as dolphin fish or dorado, is a delicious firm fish with flesh that has a pale pink hue. This high-speed fish can grow up to 45 pounds and is a tasty catch. Mahi is best when prepared simple and fresh.

In this recipe, the action of citrus juice on the raw fish will literally "cook it," firming the flesh. The cooking process, called denaturation, is a chemical reaction between the citric acid in the fruit and the proteins in the fish. Denaturation causes the fish to become firm and opaque, almost as if it had been cooked. I love to serve this dish inside a reserved coconut shell, which turns a simple dish into something that is beautiful and sophisticated.

Note: Coconuts, ceviche marinade, fish (keep the fish and marinade separate until plating), salsa, and garnishes can be prepared in advance and stored in the refrigerator before plating.

3 whole, mature brown coconuts
9 ounces mahi mahi* or any freshly caught, semi-firm, white-fleshed ocean fish
Summer Salsa (recipe follows)
¼ cup fresh lime juice
¼ cup fresh lemon juice
½ cup fresh orange juice
2 teaspoons liquid honey
4 teaspoons chopped cilantro
4 teaspoons minced chives
2 to 3 banana leaves, optional
3 cups salt or sand, for plating
Fresh herbs, optional
Plantain or cassava chips, optional

How to open a coconut: Hold the coconut firmly in your non-working hand over a bowl that will collect the coconut water.

Using the blunt end of a large kitchen knife, cleaver, or hammer, hit around the circumference of the narrowest part of the shell until the coconut has cracked open. This may take three or four rotations around the circumference. Try to hit in the same area each time until you see it crack. Rinse and reserve the shells with the coconut meat intact and store under a damp cloth until service.

Strain the coconut water through a cheesecloth-lined strainer or sieve. Reserve ¼ cup coconut water for the ceviche marinade.

With a sharp knife, skin mahi mahi*, remove bloodline, and cut in ½-inch cubes. Place fish in a small bowl, cover and refrigerate.

Prepare the Summer Salsa.

To prepare the marinade: in a medium bowl, whisk together reserved coconut water, lime, lemon and orange juices, honey, cilantro, and chives. Add mahi mahi* and stir to coat. Marinate 15 minutes in refrigerator until exterior has been lightly "cooked." **Note:** Serve the fish within a 15 to 30 minute timeframe so that the flesh does not continue to "cook" and become too firm.

To Plate

Remove the rib from each banana leaf. Portion the leaves into 12 pieces and place 2 leaves in the center of each serving bowl or plate. Place ½ cup of salt or sand in the center of each plate, mounding it high in the center. This will be the base to hold your coconut shells upright and rigid. Place a halved coconut, skin side down, firmly in the mound so that it sits flat and upright.

Portion the mahi mahi* between the coconut shells, filling with as much of the marinade as possible, without overflowing. Garnish with Summer Salsa, herbs, and optional plantain or cassava chips.

Serves 6

Crab Cakes

Crabs are known for their succulent, sweet meat, and though I prefer to use fresh lump crabmeat, pasteurized canned crab may also be used as a substitute.

This recipe uses ⅓ cup portions of crab to produce eight appetizer servings. Portions can vary anywhere from ⅛ cup to ½ cup depending on the use of the recipe; hors d'oeuvre, appetizer, or entrée.

Note: The jam, salsa, crab cake mixture (do not sear), and garnishes can be prepared in advance and refrigerated for plating.

Crab Cakes

Tomato Ginger Jam (recipe follows)
Summer Salsa (recipe follows)
1 pound lump crabmeat
¼ cup thinly sliced green onion
¼ cup finely diced sweet red pepper
½ cup Mayonnaise*
1 large egg
1 tablespoon Dijon mustard
1½ teaspoons fresh lemon juice
½ teaspoon salt
⅛ teaspoon white pepper
¼ teaspoon Sriracha sauce*
¼ teaspoon Worcestershire sauce*
¾ teaspoon Old Bay Seasoning* or Penzeys Bangkok Blend*
1 garlic clove, finely minced
¾ cup all-purpose flour
3 large eggs, lightly beaten
1½ cups panko*
Salt and white pepper
¼ cup vegetable oil*

Prepare the Tomato Ginger Jam and Summer Salsa.

Place crabmeat in a fine mesh strainer and press firmly to remove as much excess liquid as possible. Pick through the meat using your fingertips and remove any shells or cartilage.

In a large bowl, combine the ingredients, crabmeat through garlic. Blend well with your fingertips or spatula until thoroughly combined.

Using three separate bowls, add the flour to the first bowl, eggs to the second, and panko* in the third. Season each bowl with a large pinch of salt and white pepper.

To prepare crab cakes: using ⅓ cup portions and form 8 patties, 2-inches in diameter and 1-inch thick. Coat the patties in flour shaking to remove excess. Dip the patties in the egg and coat with the panko* crumbs, pressing to adhere.

In a large sauté pan, heat oil over medium-high heat. Test the oil by placing a piece of crab into the oil; when it begins to bubble and fry, you have reached the correct temperature. If oil begins to smoke, immediately lower the heat.

Add crab cakes to skillet and pan fry 2 to 3 minutes on each side, until crispy and golden brown.

Summer Salsa

3 tablespoons ⅛-inch diced red pepper
3 tablespoons ⅛-inch diced mango
Pinch cumin
Salt and pepper

In a small bowl, combine red pepper, mango, and cumin; season to taste with salt and pepper. Reserve in refrigerator until service.

Tomato Ginger Jam

1 teaspoon sesame oil
2 tablespoons unsalted butter
⅓ cup minced white onion
1 tablespoon minced fresh ginger
1 large garlic clove, minced
1 tablespoon granulated sugar

1½ pounds tomatoes, seeded and diced, or 14-ounce can diced tomatoes, drained
⅛ teaspoon Sriracha*
1½ tablespoons fresh lime juice
2 tablespoons chopped fresh cilantro
¼ teaspoon salt
¼ teaspoon black pepper

Heat a sauté pan over medium-high heat. When hot, add oil, butter, onion, ginger, and garlic; sauté until translucent, about 4 minutes. Add sugar and stir until dissolved. Turn heat to medium-low, add tomatoes and Sriracha* and continue to simmer another 15 minutes, stirring occasionally.

Remove from heat and stir in lime juice, cilantro, salt and pepper. Cool and reserve for service.

Salad Garnish

½ head frisée lettuce
1 teaspoon fresh lemon juice
1 tablespoon extra virgin olive oil
Salt and pepper
32 thinly sliced cucumber rounds

Pull the frisée lettuce leaves into bite-size pieces. Wash greens, drain, pat dry, and reserve in refrigerator for plating.

In a small bowl, combine lemon juice, olive oil, and salt and pepper to taste; stir to blend and reserve.

Just before service, toss greens with the lemon-olive oil mixture.

To Plate

Place a dollop of Tomato Ginger Jam on eight individual serving plates, top with a crab cake and garnish with the Summer Salsa and Salad Garnish.

Serves 8

Crab Salad with Wafer-Thin Crostini

Note: All ingredients can be prepared in advance; store in the refrigerator prior to plating. **Note:** It is easier to achieve a thin crostini when slicing a frozen, rather than fresh, baguette.

Sweet Corn Ice Cream (recipe follows)
1 pound fresh lump crabmeat (optional, pasteurized canned crab)
⅓ cup Honey Dijonnaise Dressing (see Back to Basics page 223)
¼ teaspoon Sriracha*
¼ teaspoon granulated sugar
¼ teaspoon salt
½ teaspoon fresh lemon juice
½ frozen baguette
1 tablespoon extra virgin olive oil
Salt and pepper
½ head frisée lettuce
8 cherry tomatoes, thinly sliced

Preheat oven to 375°F/190°C.

Prepare the Sweet Corn Ice Cream at least 24 hours in advance.

Place crabmeat in a fine mesh strainer and press firmly to remove as much excess liquid as possible. Pick through the meat using your fingertips and remove any shells or cartilage.

Prepare the Honey Dijonnaise Dressing.
In a bowl, combine crab, Honey Dijonnaise Dressing, Sriracha*, sugar, salt, and lemon juice; stir to combine and refrigerate until service.

Thinly slice frozen baguette on the bias to create the crostini. Arrange slices (do not overlap) on a parchment or Silpat*-lined baking sheet; drizzle with olive oil and season with salt and pepper. Bake for 5 to 7 minutes or until crisp and golden.

Transfer crostini to baking rack, cool, and reserve for service. If preparing in advance, cool and store in an airtight container for up to one week.

Pull the frisée lettuce leaves into bite-size pieces. Wash greens, drain, pat dry, and reserve in refrigerator for plating.

To Plate

Remove Sweet Corn Ice Cream from freezer to soften for service. If using a Pacojet*, pacotize the ice cream reserved in the beaker.

Portion and spoon the crab mixture into eight individual bowls; garnish with frisée, cherry tomatoes and 2 crostini. Serve the Sweet Corn Ice Cream in a quenelle* like shape alongside the crab or in a small individual dish.

Serves 8

Sweet Corn Ice Cream

½ cup whole milk (3.25% M.F.)
½ cup heavy cream (36% M.F.)
1¼ cups sweet yellow corn kernels
¾ teaspoon granulated sugar
¼ teaspoon white pepper
Pinch salt

Combine all ingredients in a small saucepan, stir and bring to boil. Immediately remove from heat and allow mixture to cool.

In a blender, purée mixture until smooth. Strain mixture through a sieve and place in an ice cream/sorbet maker or Pacojet* cylinder and follow manufacturer's directions to make the ice cream.

Jerk-Rubbed Chilean Sea Bass
with Tuna Tartar

I first created this dish to highlight my newfound passion for the flavors of the Caribbean. This dish is a mélange of Caribbean flavors and can be created into a starter or a main event. The first time I executed this dish was for the chef competition at the British Virgin Islands Boat Show. At this show, the yacht and her crew won best appetizer, best overall dish, best crew, and best charter yacht of the year.

Advanced Prep (up to 12 hours before service)

Chilean Sea Bass

Soy Glaze (see Back to Basics page 228)
Cilantro Oil (see Back to Basics page 218)
1 Chilean sea bass fillet (16 ounces)
1½ tablespoons all-purpose flour
1 large egg, lightly beaten
1 teaspoon jerk seasoning*
3 tablespoons panko breadcrumbs*
Salt and white pepper
1 tablespoon sesame oil

Prepare the Soy Glaze and Cilantro Oil.

Using a 2-inch round cookie cutter, portion the sea bass fillet into 6 rounds, each weighing 1½ to 2 ounces. The round will imitate the shape of a scallop. Place portions on a paper towel-lined plate to absorb moisture and refrigerate for service.

Using three separate bowls, add the flour to the first bowl, egg to the second, and the seasoning and panko* in the third. Season each bowl with a large pinch of salt and white pepper and reserve for service.
Note: Complete the following step just before service to ensure the coating is fresh.

Bread only the flat ends of each sea bass round so that you do not conceal the beautiful color and texture of the fish in the finished product. Coat each end in flour and brush off excess.

Dip the ends in the egg wash and finish ends in the seasoned panko* mixture, pressing to adhere.

Polenta

1½ cups coconut milk
1¼ cups vegetable or chicken broth
½ teaspoon minced garlic
¾ cup quick cooking polenta*
¼ cup unsalted butter
2 tablespoons cream cheese
2 tablespoons minced chives
½ teaspoon salt
⅛ teaspoon white pepper
4 tablespoons all-purpose flour
1 tablespoon extra virgin olive oil
1 tablespoon butter (2nd amount)

Add coconut milk, broth, and garlic to a heavy-bottomed saucepan and bring to a boil over medium-high heat. Reduce heat to low and whisking constantly, gradually pour the polenta* into the liquid. Continue to whisk until smooth and no lumps are visible, cover and stir every 1 to 2 minutes, until cooked and thickened, about 5 minutes.

Remove from heat, add butter, cream cheese, and chives, stir to combine. Adjust seasoning with salt and white pepper.

Immediately spread the polenta* into a lightly-buttered 9-inch round baking pan, level, smooth top and cool. When at room temperature, cover with plastic wrap and refrigerate until firm.

Before service, remove polenta* from refrigerator and cut into 2-inch rounds. Dust with flour and reserve for service.

Plantain

½ ripe plantain (yellow with minimal brown flecks)
3 tablespoons sesame oil, divided
Salt and pepper

Peel and slice plantain into ¼-inch thick rounds. Soak rounds in water, just enough to cover, for 15 minutes.

Note: This allows the plantain's starch and gluten to soften and create a creamy, smooth-textured product.

Remove plantain from water and pat dry with paper towel to remove extra moisture.

Heat 1½ tablespoons sesame oil in a sauté pan over medium heat, add the rounds and cook 2 minutes per side. Remove from pan and smash each round with a heavy flat surface to create a 2-inch flat pancake-shaped patty; reserve on counter for service.

Mango Papaya Salsa

2 tablespoons ⅛-inch diced mango
2 tablespoons ⅛-inch diced papaya
1 tablespoon ⅛-inch diced red onion
2 tablespoons thinly sliced cherry tomato
1 teaspoon chopped cilantro
¼ teaspoon cumin
½ teaspoon lime juice
¼ teaspoon minced garlic
1 teaspoon extra virgin olive oil
Salt to taste

In a small bowl, add all ingredients and stir to combine. Cover and refrigerate to allow flavors to marry before service.

Tuna Tartar

1 tablespoon Mayonnaise (see Back to Basics page 224)
½ teaspoon Sriracha*
Salt and white pepper
4 ounces fresh sashimi-grade tuna

In a small bowl, combine Mayonnaise and Sriracha*; season with salt and white pepper to taste.
Note: You may alter the level of spiciness to your likening using more or less Sriracha*.

Dice tuna uniformly into ¼-inch cubes and thoroughly incorporate in the Sriracha* mixture. Cover and refrigerate for service.

Garnish

½ semi-firm avocado
6 cilantro leaves

Just prior to service, thinly slice the avocado to use as a garnish. Form the avocado into the shape of a rose, if desired.

Reserve cilantro leaves in the refrigerator for garnish.

Service

Thirty minutes before service, remove fish from the refrigerator and bring to room temperature.

For the Fish: once the fish has been breaded, heat a 10-inch skillet over medium-high heat. When hot, add 1 tablespoon sesame oil. Add fish and sear one side undisturbed for 2 to 3 minutes. Using tongs, turn the fish and sear the second side for 2 to 3 minutes, or until firm to the touch and fish is fully cooked.

For the Polenta*: heat a medium sauté pan over medium-high heat with 1 tablespoon olive oil and 1 tablespoon butter. Add the flour-dusted polenta* rounds and sear until golden brown on each side.

For the Plantain: heat 1½ tablespoons sesame oil in a sauté pan over medium-high heat. Add the plantain patties and sauté until heated thoroughly and browned on each side, about 3 to 4 minutes.

To Plate

On each of six serving plates, place the polenta* round as a base, stack with the sea bass and plantain chip and top with salsa and cilantro leaf. Beside the stack, place the Tuna Tartar and a garnish of thinly sliced avocado. To finish: place a pool of Cilantro Oil around the base of the polenta* and garnish with the Soy Glaze.

Serves 6

Prawn Cocktail

There are hundreds of species of shrimp and prawns found in salt and fresh bodies of water around the world. Both shrimp and prawns are graded using their count per weight. Ranging from extra small to extra colossal, they are measured by kilo or pound. The numbers normally range U (under) 5 per pound to 62/69 pieces per pound. For this recipe I use 16/20 prawns per pound.

Note: All ingredients can be prepared up to 12 hours prior to service.

32 raw prawns, peeled, deveined, and tails intact
Court Bouillon (see Back to Basics page 219), use full recipe
Blush Cocktail Sauce (recipe follows)
8 cherry tomatoes
3 cups chiffonade* lettuce
8 lemon slices
2 stalks celery, thinly cut on bias
16 Belgian endive leaves (optional)
Fresh herbs of choice

In a stockpot, bring Court Bouillon to boil and reduce to simmer. Add prawns and poach until just cooked, about 5 to 6 minutes. Using a slotted spoon, remove prawns to a baking sheet and cool. When cooled, cover and refrigerate for plating.

Prepare the Blush Cocktail Sauce, cover and refrigerate for plating. With a serrated knife, cut an X in the pointed end of each cherry tomato being careful not to cut all the way through. Gently pull the tomato apart to create a flower; cover and refrigerate for plating.

To Plate

Equally portion lettuce chiffonade* into eight flared cocktail glasses (martini glasses). Place a tomato flower on the chiffonade* in each glass. Cut a slit in each lemon slice; hang one lemon slice and 4 prawns on the rim of each glass.

Creatively arrange celery and endive to "stand tall" in each glass and finish with a garnish of fresh herbs. Pour Blush Cocktail Sauce into eight small side dishes for dipping.

Serves 8

Blush Cocktail Sauce

½ cup tomato ketchup
⅓ cup Mayonnaise (see Back to Basics page 224)
¼ teaspoon Worcestershire sauce*
¼ teaspoon prepared horseradish*
1 teaspoon granulated sugar
½ teaspoon Old Bay Seasoning*
¼ teaspoon Sriracha*
1 teaspoon fresh lemon juice
Salt and white pepper

In a bowl, combine first 8 ingredients and blend until smooth. Adjust seasoning with salt and white pepper to taste. Refrigerate until service.

Yields ¾ cup

Salmon Gravlax preparation

Salmon Gravlax

This salmon gravlax is wonderful served as a canapé, appetizer, or paired with a salad for lunch.

Advanced Prep (gravlax will need to be prepared 2 to 3 days before service to ensure the fillet is fully cured)

Note: The gravlax can be prepared and frozen for up to 2 to 3 months.

1 teaspoon pink peppercorns
1 teaspoon coriander seeds
2 teaspoons juniper berries
3 tablespoons coarse sea salt
1½ tablespoons granulated sugar
1 pound fresh, antibiotic-free sustainable salmon, skin-on and descaled
½ cup coarsely chopped fresh dill
½ cup coarsely chopped fresh cilantro
Watercress Dressing (recipe follows)

Heat a small dry sauté pan over medium-high heat; add the peppercorns and coriander seeds, while frequently shaking the sauté pan, cook until spices are fragrant, about 1-2 minutes. Remove spices from heat; combine with the juniper berries and cool. Place spices in a mortar with pestle and crush. Alternatively, transfer cooled spices to a work surface, cover with kitchen towel (not terry cloth) and crush with a mallet or bottom of a heavy pan. Transfer spices to a small bowl; add salt and sugar and reserve for curing.
Place salmon fillet, skin side down, on a clean cutting board and

run your fingertips lightly along the surface to feel if there are pin bones. If bones are present, remove them with a pair of tweezers or small pliers. Grasp the tip of the bone and pull firmly on an angle to remove; repeat for remaining bones.

Flip the fillet skin side up and using a small sharp knife, poke 12 small holes through the skin.
Rub ⅓ of the spice mixture over skin. Sprinkle half of the chopped dill and cilantro into the bottom of a glass or ceramic dish large enough to hold the salmon fillet in a single layer. Place salmon, skin side down, on top of the chopped dill and cilantro. Rub remaining spice mixture into the flesh of the salmon and top with remaining chopped dill and cilantro. Using plastic wrap, cover the fillet and press the wrap directly onto the surface. Place a plate or smaller baking dish directly onto the plastic wrapped salmon. Position two 14-ounce cans onto the flat surface to act as weights for the curing process.

Refrigerate the salmon and weights for 12 hours or overnight. After 12 hours, remove from the fridge, unwrap the fish and discard any liquid that has accumulated in the bottom of the dish. Flip the salmon so it is skin side up, cover with plastic wrap in the same fashion as before; add the weights and return to the refrigerator for an additional 12 hours. Repeat this process 2 additional times for a total of 2 days (48 hours) of curing time.

Note: This will give you a medium cure.

If you desire a firmer texture with saltier taste it is possible to cure for an additional day, for a total of up to three days of curing time. Once the curing process is complete, remove the salmon from the fridge discard the curing mixture and herbs. Prepare an ice bath by combining ice and water in a large bowl. Dunk fillet into the ice bath and lightly rinse the remaining cure from the surface. Remove fillet from the ice bath and pat dry. Cover and refrigerate for service.

Note: This process can be completed up to three days prior to service.

Prepare Watercress Dressing.

Garnish

2 celery stalks
1 small English cucumber
6 frisée leaves
18 sprigs parsley or micro greens
6 edible flowers
1 small sweet potato
2 cups vegetable oil*
Salt and freshly cracked black pepper

Trim celery stalks and thinly slice lengthwise with a vegetable peeler.

Reserve strips in a bowl of ice water to create a curled effect for the garnish.

Halve the cucumber lengthwise and remove seeds. Using a vegetable peeler, thinly slice cucumber lengthwise to make 6 thin slices.

Roll each slice into a round. Cover with a damp paper towel and refrigerate for plating.

Rinse frisée and parsley sprigs, pat dry, and refrigerate for plating.

Using a vegetable peeler, remove skin from the sweet potato and discard. Thinly slice potato lengthwise into thin strips for frying.

Heat oil in a heavy bottomed saucepan until oil reaches 266°F/130°C. Adding ¼-cup sweet potato at a time, fry potatoes until the bubbles subside and potatoes are crisp. With a slotted spoon, remove potatoes to a paper towel-lined plate and season with salt and pepper.

Service

Place the salmon on a cutting board and using a very sharp knife, slice the gravlax on the bias into thin slices for service.

To Plate

I prefer to use square plates for the presentation of this dish, but any shape and size can be used. Fan 4 to 5 slices of gravlax into the center of each plate. Garnish the dish with celery curls, cucumber round, frisée, parsley sprigs, edible flower, and sweet potato chips.

To finish: drizzle with the Watercress Dressing.

Serves 6

Watercress Dressing

1 tablespoon Mayonnaise (see Back to Basics page 224)
½ ounce (⅓ cup packed) watercress
½ teaspoon fresh lemon juice
1½ teaspoons chopped cilantro
1½ tablespoons water
Pinch sugar
Pinch salt
2 tablespoons vegetable oil*

Prepare the mayonnaise in advance. Prepare an ice bath in advance by combining ice and water in a small bowl.

Bring a small saucepan of salted water to a boil (1½ tablespoons salt per quart of water). Add watercress and blanch 15 seconds. Drain and immediately plunge leaves into ice bath to stop the cooking process and retain the vibrant green color. Strain leaves and squeeze as much of the water out as possible. If water remains, wrap the leaves in a paper towel, squeeze, and wring to remove excess water.

Using a food processor or blender, combine Mayonnaise, watercress, lemon juice, cilantro, water, sugar, and salt. Turn the speed to high, remove the top of the blender or food processor and slowly add the oil in a steady stream. Blend until the dressing is thoroughly emulsified, about 3 to 4 minutes. Transfer to a squeeze bottle for service.

Trio of Tuna

Sushi or sashimi-grade fish is a label for high-quality seafood that was created as a marketing tool, not a term associated with how the product was handled or that the product has the ability to be consumed raw. With this in mind, always ensure that the source and quality of your seafood is safe for raw consumption. I highly recommend the company *SeafoodS.com*, and have been using the company for years as my number one source for quality seafood. Mike Casagrande from *SeafoodS.com* will help you choose the best quality seafood for your needs and have it delivered it straight to your door.

Advanced Prep (up to 12 hours before service)

Tuna Nigiri

6 slices sashimi-grade tuna, 1 ounce each
6 tablespoons cooked Black Heirloom Rice (recipe follows); option: cooked sticky coconut rice or cooked sushi rice
3 teaspoons Citrus Caviar (see Molecular Caviars in Back to Basics page 224)
6 dill leaves

Trim each slice of tuna into a ½-inch thick, 2¼ x 1¼-inch rectangle. Reserve refrigerated for service.

Prepare the rice and caviar. Rinse dill leaves; pat dry and refrigerate for plating.

Smoked Tuna in Cucumber Shell

1 whole 4-ounce piece sashimi-grade tuna
1 teaspoon cherrywood smoking chips (optional)
1 tablespoon Mayonnaise (see Back to Basics page 224)
½ teaspoon Sriracha*
1 English cucumber, 10 to 12-inches long and ½-inch width
6 chervil, micro basil, or micro radish leaves

To smoke the tuna (optional): with a paper towel, pat tuna dry and place in a lidded airtight container. Follow the directions for a smoking gun that is using cherrywood chips. When the gun begins to smoke, crack the lid of the tuna container and fill the chamber with smoke. Immediately seal the container and "smoke" the tuna for 3 minutes. Remove the tuna and slice in ¼-inch cubes.

In a bowl, combine the Mayonnaise and Sriracha* and stir thoroughly. Add the tuna to the Sriracha* aioli and gently toss, ensuring that you do not damage the flesh. Cover and refrigerate for service.

Using a vegetable peeler, cut lengthwise strips, evenly apart, from the four exterior sides of the cucumber. Cut and discard the ends of the cucumber. Slice the cucumber into 12 separate ¾-inch rounds. Using a small melon baller* or spoon, scoop out a shallow bowl shape in the top of each cucumber round leaving the walls intact. Place rounds in a bowl, cover with a damp paper towel and refrigerate for service.

Refrigerate chervil or micro greens for plating.

Tuna Tataki

1 sashimi-grade tuna steak (6 to 10 ounces)
2 tablespoons liquid honey
1½ teaspoons tamari* or soy sauce
¾ teaspoon Dijon mustard
¾ teaspoon grainy mustard
1½ teaspoons sesame oil
2 tablespoons black sesame seeds
½ teaspoon Old Bay Seasoning* or Penzeys Bangkok Blend*
⅛ teaspoon salt
1 tablespoon sesame oil (2nd amount)
¼ cup micro greens
1 tablespoon pickled sushi ginger
1 teaspoon of wasabi

With a paper towel, pat tuna dry; cover and reserve on counter.

In a small bowl, combine honey, tamari*, mustards, and 1½ teaspoons of sesame oil; whisk thoroughly to combine.

Add sesame seeds, Bangkok Blend* and salt on a small plate and blend with your fingertips to combine. Coat all sides of the tuna with the sesame seed mixture.

Heat a small sauté pan over medium-high heat and when hot, add 1 tablespoon sesame oil (2nd amount). Add tuna to the pan and sear 45 to 60 seconds per side. This searing method results in an ideal, very rare tuna.

Refrigerate micro greens for plating.

Black Heirloom Rice

⅓ cup black Burmese rice
⅓ cup coconut milk
⅓ cup water
½ teaspoon salt

Combine all ingredients in a small heavy-bottomed saucepan. Bring to a boil, lower heat, cover, and simmer 40 minutes.

Remove from heat and reserve, covered, an additional 10 minutes.

Transfer rice to a baking sheet and spread in a thin layer for rapid cooling. Cover baking sheet with plastic wrap and reserve on counter to room temperature.

Service

For the Tuna Nigiri: mold the Black Heirloom Rice into six, 1 tablespoon-size quenelle* shapes to form a base. Top each quenelle* with a slice of the tuna.

For the Smoked Tuna in Cucumber Shell: fill each cucumber cup evenly with the cubed tuna.

For the Tuna Tataki: place the seared tuna onto a clean cutting board and thinly slice into 12 portions.

To Plate

To present this dish, I prefer to use rectangular wooden, sushi, or white plates.

Starting on the right section of the plate, place one portion of the Tuna Nigiri and garnish with a dill leaf and caviar.

In the center of the plate, place two of the cucumber cups in a row and garnish with micro leaves.

On the left side of the plate, using a pastry brush, "paint" the honey mixture onto the base of the plate. Top the brush stroke with two portions of Tuna Tataki; overlap one another and garnish with micro greens.

Repeat process for remaining plates.

Portion additional pickled ginger, wasabi, soy sauce, and the remaining honey mixture into four ramekins to accompany the service.

Serves 6

S/Y Wonderful stern-to in one of our favorite anchorages, Cumberland Bay, Saint Vincent and the Grenadines. Here I would wake each morning to find gifts of fresh fruit and herbs, picked straight from the rainforest in the morning dew and left on the stern for us to enjoy.

This bay is also home to our friend Brazil Scarborough, AKA "Brother." Brother is one of those individuals who has made such an impression on our life that we consider him family. A dear friend, he ventured afar to help us achieve our goal with our own yacht, *M/S Lady Elizabeth*, in Turkey. His dedication, endurance, and patience helped make one of our lifelong dreams a reality.

Sunrise in the middle of the Atlantic

SOUPS

Carrot and Ginger Soup

Healthy, delicious, and velvety, this versatile carrot and ginger soup is perfect for any occasion. It can be served hot or cold, and I must admit that I love it chilled as it is so light and refreshing. If serving chilled, refrigerate at least two hours before service.

Note: This soup can be made well in advance or frozen for later use.

Balsamic Vinegar Pearls (see Back to Basics page 213)
Citrus Caviar (see Back to Basics page 224)
Crostini (see recipe page 115)
2 tablespoons unsalted butter
1½ pounds ½-inch dice carrot
½ cup ¼-inch dice sweet white onion
1½ teaspoons salt
2 tablespoons minced fresh ginger
1 teaspoon orange zest
2 cups chicken or vegetable broth
2¼ cups water

Prepare the Balsamic Vinegar Pearls, Citrus Caviar, and Crostini.

Melt butter in a saucepan over medium heat. Add carrots, onion, and salt to saucepan and sauté vegetables, stirring occasionally, until they are softened but not browned, about 10 minutes.

Add ginger, orange zest, broth, and water to saucepan; bring to boil and reduce to simmer. Cook until carrots are tender, about 20 minutes.

Remove saucepan from cooktop. Use an immersion blender to purée soup to desired consistency or use a traditional blender and purée soup in batches. If you desire a thinner soup, add a little water or broth to the purée.

Adjust seasoning and serve with the crostini topped with Citrus Caviar and Balsamic Vinegar Pearls.

Serves 6

Cauliflower and Fennel Emulsion

Note: This soup can be made well in advance or frozen for later use.

Balsamic Vinegar Pearls (see Back to Basics page 213)
4 cups 1-inch pieces cauliflower
2 cups ½-inch dice fennel
1 cup ½-inch dice white onion
3½ cups vegetable or chicken broth
1 teaspoon herbes de Provence*
1½ teaspoons salt
¼ teaspoon white pepper
½ cup Boursin* cheese, crumbled
2 teaspoons extra virgin olive oil
8 large scallops, about ½ to ¾ pound
¼ teaspoon salt (2nd amount)
⅛ teaspoon white pepper
1 chive stem, 5-inch length

Prepare the Balsamic Vinegar Pearls.

Combine the seven ingredients (cauliflower to white pepper) in a stockpot; bring
to boil, reduce to simmer, and cook until vegetables are tender, about 10 minutes.
Remove from heat, add Boursin cheese* and stir to combine.

In a blender, purée soup in batches until smooth. Return soup to stockpot, adjust seasoning, and bring to serving temperature.

Heat a large skillet on medium-high heat; add olive oil and sear scallops 1 to 1½ minutes on each side until golden brown.
Remove scallops from pan and season with salt and white pepper.

Cut chive stem into eight ½-inch pieces for garnish.

To Plate

Ladle soup into wide, shallow soup bowls so that soup depth is about 1 inch. Add a scallop to the center of each bowl. The shallow
depth of the soup enables the scallop to be visible. Garnish with Balsamic Vinegar Pearls, chives, and smoked sea salt. The additional
garnish found in the photograph for this recipe is a potato spiral cannoli and baby arugula.

Serves 8

Frothy Lobster Bisque

For this recipe I use North Atlantic lobster, which is readily available internationally and sourced from Atlantic Canada and the American state of Maine. I prefer to use the tail and claw meat from 1 to 2 pound lobsters, as this size will yield the sweetest and most tender flesh.

Note: This bisque can be made well in advance or frozen for later use. The lobster salad, sweet corn purée, herbed panko, and garnish can be prepared up to 12 hours prior to service.

Lobster Salad

8 uncooked lobster claws
2 quarts Court Bouillon (see Back to Basics page 219)
1 tablespoon Mayonnaise (see Back to Basics page 224)
2 teaspoons ketchup
2 teaspoons grainy mustard
½ teaspoon Old Bay Seasoning*
½ teaspoon Worcestershire sauce*
Pinch of sugar
Salt and pepper
Micro greens, for garnish

Remove lobster claws from refrigerator and bring to room temperature. In a large heavy-bottomed saucepan, bring Court Bouillon to a boil, add claws and poach 5 minutes

Using a slotted spoon, remove claws from Court Bouillon and allow claws to cool. Remove meat from the shells and finely dice the meat. Reserve shells for the Lobster Bisque.

In a small bowl, combine Mayonnaise, ketchup, mustard, Old Bay*, Worcestershire* sauce, and sugar; stir until smooth. Add diced lobster to mixture and adjust seasoning with salt and pepper. Cover and refrigerate for service.

Reserve micro greens in refrigerator for plating.

Lobster Bisque

2 tablespoons extra virgin olive oil
1 medium onion, peeled and chopped
1 large carrot, peeled and chopped
2 leeks, trimmed, cleaned and chopped
4 garlic cloves, peeled
Small handful of herb sprigs (coriander, parsley, basil, etc.)
6 pink peppercorns
6 star anise* pods
2 tablespoons tomato purée
1 cup cognac
1 cup dry white wine, *Hahn Pinot Gris*
3 cups seafood or chicken broth
3 lobster claw shells (reserved from Lobster Salad)
⅔ cup heavy cream (36% M.F.)
2 tablespoons Roux* (see Back to Basics page 228)
Salt and pepper

In a stockpot, heat olive oil over medium-high heat; add onion, carrot, leeks, and garlic and sauté until lightly browned, about 3 to 4 minutes. Add herb sprigs, peppercorns, and star anise* to stockpot; stir in tomato purée and cook 3 minutes.

Add cognac to stockpot and flambé, being careful not to burn yourself. When the flambé dies, add wine to stockpot and reduce 10 minutes. Add stock and lobster shells to stockpot and simmer 20 minutes.

To finish: strain the soup through a fine mesh sieve into a clean heavy-bottomed saucepan. Return saucepan to heat, add cream and whisk in Roux* until desired consistency is achieved. Adjust seasoning with salt and pepper to taste and reserve for service.

Sweet Corn Purée

1 can corn kernels, drained (15 ounce)
1 tablespoon butter
3 tablespoons heavy cream (36% M.F.)
3 tablespoons chicken stock
Pinch sugar
Pinch salt and white pepper

In a small saucepan, add all ingredients and heat until almost a boil. Remove from heat and transfer corn mixture to a blender. Purée corn until smooth; strain through a sieve and reserve.

Herbed Panko (garnish)

½ cup packed basil leaves
½ cup panko breadcrumbs*
Salt

Prepare ice bath in advance by combining ice and water in a small bowl.

In a small saucepan, bring liberally salted water to a boil (1½ tablespoons salt per quart of water); add basil leaves and blanch 15 seconds. Drain and immediately plunge leaves into ice bath to stop the cooking process and retain the vibrant green color. Remove leaves from ice bath and squeeze leaves to remove as much of the water as possible.

In a food processor, combine the panko*, basil leaves, and pinch of salt. Pulse until the panko* and basil are thoroughly combined and resemble green sand; reserve for plating.

Service

Remove the lobster salad from refrigerator 30 minutes before service.

In separate saucepans, heat the Lobster Bisque and Sweet Corn Purée over medium heat until thoroughly heated.

Froth the Lobster Bisque using a pumping action with a hand blender.

To Plate

I use wide rimmed soup bowls to accentuate the presentation of this dish. Sprinkle the Herbed Panko*, as garnish, on the rim of soup bowl.
Place a 2-inch ring mold in the center of the bowl and press 1 to 2 tablespoons of the lobster salad into the mold creating a compact round. Remove the ring mold and top the lobster with micro greens and Sweet Corn Purée. Repeat for remaining bowls.

It is optional to use four 4- to 6-ounce cream pitchers to serve the bisque portion of the recipe.

Note: If using pitchers, we recommend that the pitchers have a handle as the bisque may be very hot.

If not using the cream pitchers, ladle the bisque around the lobster. If using the cream pitchers, ladle the lobster bisque into the pitchers and serve with the lobster dish.

Serves 4

Prawn Chowder

Lovers of creamy chowders will adore this version featuring fresh vegetables and charred prawns.

Note: This chowder can be made up to 12 hours before plating.

⅔ cup diced, uncooked bacon
1 cup ⅛-inch diced sweet onion
1 cup ⅛-inch diced carrot
½ cup ⅛-inch diced celery
2 tablespoons tomato paste
½ cup dry white wine, *Hahn Pinot Gris*
3 cups broth (seafood, chicken, or vegetable)
1½ cups ⅛-inch diced potato
1 cup fresh yellow corn
2 bay leaves
2½ teaspoons dried Italian herbs
1 tablespoon granulated sugar
1 cup heavy cream (36% M.F.)
1 tablespoon extra-virgin olive oil
2 teaspoons smoked paprika
1 teaspoon minced garlic
¼ teaspoon salt
⅛ teaspoon white pepper
16 prawns, peeled and deveined (16-20 count)
Fresh herbs of choice
Tortilla Chips (recipe follows)

In a large saucepan over medium-high heat, sauté bacon until crisp. Lower heat to medium; add onion, carrot, and celery and cook, stirring occasionally, until onions are softened, about 5 minutes. Add tomato paste to mixture and stir to combine.

Add wine to saucepan, raise heat to high and stir to scrape up bits from bottom of pan. Stir in stock and add potato, corn, and bay leaves. Reduce heat to simmer and cook until potatoes are barely tender, about 6 minutes. Add Italian herbs and sugar; continue cooking, stirring occasionally, on low simmer for 20 minutes.

Stir in cream; remove bay leaves and bring to serving temperature, being careful not to boil.

In a bowl, combine olive oil, smoked paprika, garlic, salt, and white pepper. Add prawns and lightly toss to coat. Bring a skillet to medium-high heat; add prawns and sauté until cooked, about 3 minutes per side.

To Plate

Ladle chowder into warmed soup bowls, top with prawns and garnish with fresh herbs and Tortilla Chips.

Serves 8

Tortilla Chips

1 8-inch white flour tortilla
½ cup vegetable oil*
Salt and pepper

Cut tortilla into 8 triangles. Heat oil in a medium skillet over medium-high heat until oil reaches 266°F/130°C. Adding one triangle at a time, fry tortilla until golden brown; remove with tongs and place on paper towels to remove excess oil.

Repeat process for each tortilla triangle. Season with salt and pepper to taste.

Roasted Carrot and Brie Bisque

I find this dish also works beautifully served as an hors d'oeuvre; simply fill a shot glass and serve with a Brie crostini and fresh herbs.

Note: This soup can be made well in advance or frozen for later use.

2 pounds 1-inch pieces of carrot
1 large sweet onion, ½-inch slices, separated
½ head garlic, cloves separated and peeled
5 stalks celery, cut in 1-inch pieces
¼ ounce fresh thyme sprigs (10 to 12 sprigs)
3 tablespoons extra virgin olive oil
Salt and black pepper
4 cups chicken or vegetable broth
8 ounces Brie or Camembert cheese
Crostini (recipe follows)
2 teaspoons extra virgin olive oil (2nd amount)
Fresh herbs
Tellicherry pepper*

Preheat oven to 400°F/205°C.

In a large roasting pan, arrange carrots, onion, garlic, celery, and thyme. Drizzle olive oil over vegetables and season with a generous amount of salt and freshly cracked black pepper; toss to coat.

Roast the vegetables, stirring every 10 to 15 minutes until carrots are cooked through and vegetables are caramelized, about 60 minutes. Remove roaster from oven and discard thyme sprigs.

In a large saucepan, combine roasted vegetables and broth; bring to boil, reduce to simmer and cook 5 to 10 minutes to rehydrate vegetables. Remove exterior white rind from cheese wheel; cut cheese into large pieces, add to saucepan and stir to combine.

In a blender, purée soup in batches until smooth. Return to sauce pan, adjust seasoning, and bring to serving temperature.

Prepare Crostini.

To Plate

Ladle soup into bowls, top with Crostini, drizzle with olive oil (2nd amount), dust with freshly cracked Tellicherry pepper*, and finish with fresh herbs.

Serves 8

Crostini

1 baguette
2 teaspoons extra virgin olive oil
Salt and pepper
6 ounces fresh goat cheese

Preheated oven to 400°F/204°C.

Cut baguette into 8 finger crostini that measure 6 inches long, ½-inch wide, and ½-inch tall each. Slice the ends on a bias for additional visual appeal.

Arrange crostini on a baking sheet; brush with olive oil, season with salt and pepper, and bake until golden, about 7 to 9 minutes. Remove baguette slices from oven and place on baking rack.

Crumble the goat cheese and place on the top of each crostini. Using a chef's torch, flame cheese until your choice of either blackened or golden brown. Alternatively, heat oven to broil, return cheese-topped crostini to baking sheet, place in oven and broil until golden, about 5 minutes.

Yields 8 crostini

M/S LADY ELIZABETH: CRUISING
THE TURQUOISE COAST

Warren and I first arrived in Turkey for *S/Y Wonderful's* refit in 2008 where we were welcomed with open arms. Here, everyone treated us like a brother or sister without knowing our names. During the winter months, living on the southwest coast was a bit like going back in time. It was peaceful and tranquil, a place where everyone still worked together as a community to make their surroundings a better place.

After years of returning to Turkey for charters and yacht repairs, we decided that it would be a wonderful place to call home. After months of searching for an ideal residence we finally thought, "Let's buy our own yacht!" We decided to purchase an 85-foot, 70-ton, 23-foot-wide investment, a project for us to create our perfect Aegean charter yacht.

After years of blood, sweat, and tears, we entered the charter circuit with our pride and joy, *Lady Elizabeth,* (formally *M/S Turkish Delight*). We had made our dream come true.

In 2015 we received a ranking with *Yachting* magazine as one of the top 10 Mediterranean charter yachts. This was a huge feat for us, having built our charter company from the ground up. The same year, I won first place Appetizer, Entrée, Dessert, and First Place Overall at the Marmaris Yacht Show Chef Competition. We were fully booked for every charter season, cruising the beautiful Turquoise Coast of southern Turkey, enjoying its amazing beauty and abundance of ancient history and culture.

Then politics and history changed our fortunes. ISIS invaded Syria, travel bans were put in place, and Syrian refugees started flooding the banks of the Aegean Sea. Words cannot express the sadness and helplessness everyone felt for these poor innocent people. It became an all too frequent and heart wrenching scene of clothing, back packs, life jackets, and overturned boats dotting the Aegean Sea. I found myself pondering over whether the men, women, children, and babies actually survived the crossing of that sometimes treacherous sea.

It was at this time that we decided to use *Lady Elizabeth* to transport relief and aid to those in need. We developed a fundraiser and supported a large group of refugees who were located very close to Turkey on the island of Kos, Greece. This was a stressful and emotional, yet incredibly rewarding experience.

The next season, after many charter cancellations, we decided to change our location to the northern Greek islands of the Sporades. If you have ever seen the movie *Mama Mia,* that is the Sporades portrayed perfectly. What a marvelous experience.

We spent the summer cruising its idyllic waters. En-route home to Turkey, we sailed south through the Cyclades, and one of my dreams came true. It was an experience I will never forget as we sailed into the open caldera of the island of Santorini with homes and hotels teetering on the cliffs like white clouds dancing on the rocks above. Santorini is a magical place full of wonder and grace.

After a multitude of emotions, to close our final season we waved goodbye to Greece and Turkey looking forward to a new chapter as it was time to find other work opportunities and a new yacht.

Entrées

Seven Hours of Roasted Leg of Lamb
(Sept Heures d'Agneau)

This version of a classic French dish is exceptionally deliciousand, and although the seven hours may discourage you, it is relatively easy to prepare. The finished product is a rich, deep, delectable dish that is sure to please any palate.

Advanced Prep (8 to 12 hours before service)

Lamb

1 bone-in leg of lamb (3 to 4 pounds)
2 tablespoons extra virgin olive oil
3¼ cups beef broth
3¼ cups (750 ml) dry white wine, *Hahn Pinot Gris*
1 cup cognac
4 medium-size carrots
2 small onions
2 medium leeks, white part only
10 medium mushrooms
4 bay leaves
4 sprigs fresh rosemary

Preheat oven to 325°F/165°C.

Remove lamb from packaging; pat dry and at the ball joint of the leg, cut and separate into two pieces.

In a Dutch oven or ovenproof* stockpot large enough to hold all ingredients, heat the oil on medium-high heat; add the lamb and sear on all sides until it retains a dark brown hue. Remove the lamb to a plate and reserve. Keeping the stockpot at the same temperature, add the stock, wine, and cognac and deglaze* the pan, scraping the brown bits from the bottom of the pan. Return the lamb to the stockpot.

Peel and cut the carrots into 4-inch segments; skin and halve the leeks and onions, trim and leave the mushrooms whole. Add the vegetables, bay leaves, and rosemary to the pot and cover. Remove to preheated oven and cook for seven hours.

Check every two hours for the first six hours and twice during the last hour to ensure the lamb is always submerged.

After seven hours, remove stockpot from oven to countertop; remove the lid and let the contents cool until it can be properly handled. When cool, strain the meat and vegetables from the pot, and reserve the strained liquid for the demi-glace. Slice the vegetables into bite-size pieces, transfer to a casserole dish, cover and reserve for service.

Remove the meat from the bone discarding the fat and bones, place in a separate ovenproof* pan, cover and reserve for service.

Lamb Demi-Glace

5 tablespoons butter
½ cup + ½ teaspoon all-purpose flour
5 cups reserved liquid from the stockpot
2 tablespoons cognac (optional)
5 tablespoons oyster sauce*
1 teaspoon Worcestershire sauce*

In a small heavy-bottomed saucepan, heat butter over medium heat until melted. Add the flour and whisk to make a roux*; continue to cook, stirring constantly for 1 minute, until a blond roux* is achieved. Remove from heat and add the stockpot liquid in a steady stream, whisking constantly to avoid lumps. Continue to cook on low heat at a steady simmer until the desired consistency is achieved, about 8 to 12 minutes.

Stir the cognac, oyster sauce*, and Worcestershire* into the glace. Pour ½ cup of the warm glace into the shredded lamb for added flavor and texture; cover and reserve for service. Reserve the remaining demi-glace in a covered saucepan.

Note: Portion and freeze the leftover demi-glace for future use.

Yields 5 cups

Green Beans

Blanching beans brightens the color and helps retain vitamins. For presentation, allow at least 7 to 8 beans per serving.

1 pound French green beans
2 teaspoons extra virgin olive oil
Salt and pepper

Prepare ice bath in advance by combining ice and water in a large bowl.

Trim the beans at each end so they are uniform and about 3-inches in length.

In a medium saucepan, bring liberally salted water to a boil (1½ tablespoons salt per quart of water). Add beans and blanch 1 to 2 minutes until they are bright green and still crunchy. Immediately remove from heat and transfer beans to ice bath to stop the cooking process. Remove beans from ice bath after 5 minutes, pat dry and refrigerate for service.

Mashed Potatoes

3 pounds potatoes, preferably russet or Yukon Gold
⅓ cup unsalted butter, at room temperature
⅔ cup heavy cream (36% M.F.)
⅛ teaspoon white pepper
Salt

Peel potatoes and cut into 1-inch cubes. In a stockpot, add potatoes with enough cold water to cover, add salt (1½ tablespoons salt per quart of water) and bring to a boil. Reduce heat slightly and cook until potatoes are very tender when pierced with a fork. Remove potatoes from heat and strain them through a colander*. It may take 2 to 3 minutes to allow all the water to drain. Return potatoes to stockpot; add butter, cream, and pepper and mash

until the potatoes are smooth.
Adjust seasoning with salt; cover and reserve for service.

Garnish

1 small sweet potato
2 cups vegetable oil*
Salt and freshly cracked black pepper

Using a vegetable peeler, remove skin from the sweet potato and thinly slice it lengthwise into thin strips for frying.

Heat oil in a heavy-bottomed saucepan until oil reaches 266°F/130°C. Adding ¼ cup sweet potato at a time, fry potatoes until the bubbles subside and potatoes crisp. With a slotted spoon, remove potatoes to a paper towel lined plate and season with salt and pepper.

Service

Preheat oven to 400°F/205°C.

In the oven, reheat the reserved lamb for 20 to 25 minutes and the vegetables for 15 minutes.

For the Mashed Potatoes: reheat in covered stockpot over medium-low heat. Check the potatoes every few minutes and stir to ensure even heating, about 10 to 15 minutes.

For the Demi-Glace*: reheat in covered saucepan over medium-low heat. Check the sauce occasionally and stir to ensure even heating, about 10 to 12 minutes.

For the Green Beans: heat a small sauté pan over medium heat. When hot, add 2 teaspoons olive oil and green beans. Lightly sauté beans until they are warmed through and just tender, about 3 to 4 minutes. Remove from heat and season with salt and pepper.

To Plate

Place a 3-inch ring mold in the center of a serving dish. Fill with the mashed potato and press to create a perfect round. Raise the ring mold 1-inch so that the top of the potato round is just below the bottom of the ring mold. Creating a second layer, gently fill the mold with the lamb and remove. Repeat the remaining steps for each of the remaining servings.

Top the lamb with the sweet potato crisps, garnish with the roasted vegetables, green beans, and demi-glace.

Serves 10

Five Spice Duck Breast

For this recipe I prefer to use White Pekin duck breasts. White Pekin ducks have tender, mild, light colored meat and are not as "gamey" as the Muscovy, Moulard, and Mallard breeds.

Advanced Prep (up to 12 hours before service)

Duck Breast

4 duck breasts, 4 to 6 ounces each
½ teaspoon five-spice powder*
⅜ teaspoon salt

Remove the sinew* from each duck breast, trim and score* the fat in a diamond pattern. Place the duck, fat side down on a paper towel-lined plate and pat dry. Rub the flesh of each breast with equal amounts of the five-spice powder and season with salt. Cover and reserve in refrigerator for service.

Sweet and Spicy Orange Glaze

1¼ cups fresh orange juice (about 3 oranges)
½ cup granulated sugar
1 tablespoon grated fresh ginger
1 small thinly sliced red chili pepper
2 teaspoons Sriracha*
2 whole star anise*
2 cinnamon sticks
1 tablespoon sweet chili sauce*
1 tablespoon Thai fish sauce*
1 tablespoon rice wine vinegar*
2 tablespoons full-bodied, fruity red wine, *Hahn GSM*

Combine all ingredients in a small saucepan and whisking occasionally, bring to a boil. Reduce heat to simmer and cook sauce until it is reduced to a syrupy consistency, about 25 to 30 minutes.

Potato Croquettes

¾ pound potatoes, preferably russet or Yukon Gold
1 tablespoon whole milk (3.25% M.F.)
⅛ cup unsalted butter
⅛ teaspoon white pepper
⅛ to ¼ teaspoon salt
2 tablespoons all-purpose flour
1 large egg, lightly beaten
6 tablespoons panko*
⅛ teaspoon dried Italian herbs
Salt and black pepper
½ teaspoon vegetable oil*
1 tablespoon unsalted butter (2nd amount)

Peel potatoes and cut into 1-inch cubes. In a stockpot, add potatoes with enough cold water to cover, add salt (1½ tablespoons salt per quart of water) and bring to a boil. Reduce heat slightly and cook until potatoes are very tender when pierced with a fork. When cooked, remove potatoes from heat and strain into a colander*. It may take 2 to 3 minutes to allow all of the water to drain.

Pass the cooked potatoes through a food mill, ricer, or sieve into the original stockpot. Stir milk and butter into the potatoes; season with white pepper and salt to taste and continue to stir until smooth and thoroughly incorporated. Cover potatoes and cool completely, before forming into 4 individual ¼-cup croquettes*.

Using three separate bowls, add flour to the first bowl, egg to the second, and panko* to the third; season each bowl with a large pinch of salt and pepper. For each croquette, coat in flour, shaking to remove excess, dip in egg, and then coat with panko* crumbs, pressing to adhere.

Heat a large sauté pan over medium heat; when hot, add ½ teaspoon oil and 1 tablespoon butter. Add croquettes to pan and sear until golden brown, about 3 to 4 minutes per side, adding additional oil if necessary. Transfer to a parchment paper or Silpat* lined baking sheet and reserve on the counter for service.

Green Beans

Blanching beans brightens the color and helps retain vitamins. For presentation, allow at least 7 or 8 beans per serving.

½ pound French green beans
2 teaspoons extra virgin olive oil
Salt and pepper

Prepare ice bath in advance by combining ice and water in a large bowl.

Trim the beans at each end so they are uniform and about 3-inches in length.

In a medium saucepan, bring liberally salted water to a boil (1½ tablespoons salt per quart of water). Add beans and blanch 1 to 2 minutes until they are bright green and still crunchy. Using a slotted spoon, transfer beans to the ice bath to stop the cooking process. After 5 minutes, remove beans from ice bath, pat dry and refrigerate for service.

Orange-Infused Fennel

½ cup freshly squeezed orange juice
1½ teaspoons liquid honey
1½ teaspoons rice wine vinegar
1 teaspoon minced chives
⅔ cup (3 ounces) fennel, thinly sliced with a mandolin*

In a bowl, combine orange juice, honey, vinegar, and chives; whisk until the honey has completely dissolved.

Place fennel in a second bowl; add the orange juice mixture to completely cover the fennel. This step allows the fennel to macerate* with the orange and honey. Cover and refrigerate for service.

Garnish

1 to 2 leeks
2 cups vegetable oil*
Salt and pepper
¼ cup micro greens

Wash leeks to make sure all grit is removed. Using only the white part of the leek(s), julienne* into ¹⁄₁₆-inch wide strips that are 2½-inches long. Prepare enough to make 1 cup.

Heat oil in a heavy-bottomed saucepan until oil reaches 266°F/130°C. Adding ¼ cup of the julienned* leeks at a time, fry until the bubbles subside and the leek is crisp. Remove with a slotted spoon, drain on a paper towel-lined plate and season with salt and pepper. Repeat procedure with remaining leek.

Reserve micro greens in the refrigerator for garnish.

Service

Preheat convection oven to 400°F/205°C.

Thirty minutes before service, remove all refrigerated items (except micro greens) and bring to room temperature.

For the Orange-Infused Fennel: strain mixture and reserve fennel in a paper towel-lined bowl for plating.

For the Potato Croquettes: reheat croquettes on a baking sheet in the oven for 10 to 12 minutes.

For the Sweet and Spicy Orange Glaze: reheat in a small saucepan over medium-low heat. Check the sauce occasionally and stir to ensure even heating.

For the Duck Breast: heat a large sauté pan over medium heat. When hot, add the duck, skin side down, and sear until the skin is evenly browned and crisp, about 8 to 9 minutes. Throughout the cooking process press the breasts with a spatula to promote even cooking and drain residual fat from the pan as necessary.

Flip the breasts and sear the flesh side 2 to 3 minutes or until the internal temperature reaches 130°F/54°C (medium-rare) or preferred doneness, remove from heat. Bear in mind that the breasts will continue to cook while resting an additional 5°F or 3 to 4°C.

For the Green Beans:: while the duck is searing, heat a medium sauté pan over medium heat. When hot, add 2 teaspoons olive oil and green beans. Lightly sauté beans until they are warmed through and just tender, about 3 to 4 minutes.

Remove from heat and season with salt and pepper.

To Plate

Place a Potato Croquette in the center of each serving plate. Top with the Green Beans and Duck Breast. Garnish with the Orange-Infused Fennel, micro greens, and crispy leek.

To finish, drizzle with the Sweet and Spicy Orange Glaze and dust with cracked pepper from a pepper grinder.

Serves 4

Short Rib Massaman Curry

I created a version of this popular Thai dish for my husband who loves Massaman curry but is not always keen on its intense peanut flavor. The result is a delicious sauce paired with incredibly tender, fall-off-the-bone short ribs. If you prefer a spicier version, add dried chilis or increase the amount of Sriracha*, and if you prefer a nuttier taste, serve with crushed peanuts on top. If possible, purchase English-style short ribs with a 2- to 4-inch bone and thick cap of surface meat.

Note: I prefer to use coconut cream for this recipe, but it is possible to substitute the cream with coconut milk. I also like to reuse the short rib braising liquid. Simply strain and substitute into any recipe that calls for beef stock or broth.

Note: The braised short ribs and Massaman sauce can be prepared and frozen up to 2 to 3 months in advance.

Short Ribs

3 to 3½ pounds bone-in beef short ribs, preferably Wagyu, if available
2 tablespoons high smoke point vegetable oil*
6 cups beef broth, divided
1 large onion cut in ½-inch rounds
2 bay leaves

Portion each short rib into three sections, each 2 x 3-inches in size.

In a large heavy-bottomed stockpot, heat oil over high heat; add small batches of short ribs at a time and briefly sear for 20 seconds per side. After each piece has been seared, remove from pan and reserve.

Note: Do not overcrowd the pan and lower the heat if the oil starts to smoke.

When the searing is complete, remove stockpot from heat and deglaze* with 2 cups of the beef broth, scraping the brown bits from the bottom of the pan. Place the seared short rib pieces, bone side down, in a single layer in the bottom of the stockpot. Cover ribs with the sliced onion, remaining beef broth and bay leaves, making sure the ribs are fully submerged in the broth. Bring stockpot to a simmer, almost to a boil, and then lower to a low simmer. Cover the pot and cook for 6 hours, ensuring that it always stays at a low simmer. **Note:** Do not stir the ribs during the cooking process.

Remove stockpot from heat and cool. While short ribs are cooling, prepare Fragrant Jasmine Rice and Massaman Curry Sauce.

Fragrant Jasmine Rice

While the rice is cooking, begin preparing the Massaman Curry Sauce.

4 cardamom pods
4 whole cloves
3 x 3-inch piece cheesecloth*
2¾ cups water
1½ cups jasmine rice
1 cinnamon stick
1 bay leaf
¾ teaspoon salt

Using a mortar and pestle or the back of a knife, gently crush the cardamom pods to release the seeds. Place cardamom pods, seeds, and cloves in the center of the cheesecloth; close and tie with twine to make a bouquet garni*.

In a medium saucepan, bring water to boil and stir in rice, bouquet garni*, cinnamon stick, bay leaf, and salt; cover and reduce the heat to low. Simmer 15 minutes or until all water has been absorbed.

Remove cooked rice from heat and keeping the cover on, set aside while you finish the dish. Discard the bouquet garni*, cinnamon, and bay leaf for service.

Massaman Curry Sauce

12 cardamom pods
2 cans coconut cream* or coconut milk
¼ cup Massaman curry paste*
1⅓ tablespoons tamarind concentrate*
2 teaspoons cumin seeds
1 teaspoon Sriracha sauce
3 tablespoons brown sugar
1½ tablespoons cornstarch
1½ tablespoons water
18 cilantro sprigs

Using a mortar and pestle or the back of a knife, gently crush the cardamom pods to release the seeds. In a heavy-bottomed saucepan, combine cardamom seeds, coconut cream*, curry paste, tamarind concentrate*, cumin seeds, Sriracha*, and brown sugar; stir to combine.

At this point, if you would like to have a medium-thick sauce, make a slurry* with the cornstarch and water in a separate bowl. Whisk until the cornstarch is completely dissolved in the water and stir into the curry sauce.

Bring the saucepan to a low simmer, making sure it does not come to a boil. Simmer 5 to 7 minutes to thicken the sauce and infuse flavors.

Remove curry sauce from heat. Remove short rib pieces from the beef broth and gently place in the curry sauce so that the meat is completely covered. Return saucepan a low-simmer to warm for service.

Note: Strain the broth used to braise the short ribs and refrigerate or freeze for later use. The broth can be used in recipes that call for stock or broth. It is a perfect addition to a traditional French onion soup!

To Plate

Divide short ribs equally between six serving dishes; cover with sauce, garnish with cilantro sprigs and serve with fragrant rice and warm naan bread.

Serves 6

Sous Vide Filet Mignon

This dish is one of my absolute favorites. I highly recommend the *sous vide method* of preparation to experience the full potential this dish has to offer. You can prepare the dish in individual portions, but my personal preference is to cook and sear the tenderloin whole. If possible, use a very hot grill to give the meat additional flavor and a wonderful "charred" effect. When sliced, the filet's beautiful pink hue is showcased and imparts a wonderful visual appeal to the dish.

Note: I prefer to use USDA Black Angus Prime, Wagyu, or Kobe beef.

Note: The uncooked tenderloin that has been marinated and sealed can, at this stage (prior to cooking), be frozen for 3 to 4 months.

Advanced Prep (up to 12 hours before service)

Filet Mignon

1 whole beef tenderloin, 16 to 20 ounces
1 teaspoon brown sugar
2 teaspoons Montreal Steak Seasoning* or Penzeys Mitchell Steak Seasoning*
2 teaspoons Worcestershire sauce*
3 tablespoons extra virgin olive oil
Bordelaise Sauce (recipe follows)

Pierce the tenderloin all over with a fork to tenderize. Rub the meat with sugar and seasoning and place in a Ziplock bag or container. Combine the Worcestershire sauce* and olive oil, pour over the meat and liberally rub it in. Seal the bag or cover the container; refrigerate for at least 4 hours and up to 2 days. If marinating for longer than 4 hours, turn at least 4 to 5 times during the marinating process.

Prepare the Bordelaise Sauce.

For the *sous vide cooking method*, follow the directions below after the steak has marinated in the refrigerator. For the *traditional cooking method*, omit this step.

SOUS VIDE METHOD
Preheat sous vide bath to 135°F/57°C or preferred internal temperature.

Prepare tenderloin for sous vide bath: place two pieces of plastic wrap, overlapping one another and lying flat on a countertop, to make an 18 x 18-inch square.

Remove tenderloin from the Ziploc bag or container and reserve 3 tablespoons of the marinade. Place tenderloin in the center of the plastic wrap and drizzle with the reserved marinade. Take the bottom seam of the plastic wrap, fold it over the top of the tenderloin and pull towards you to completely cover the meat.

Now, roll the tenderloin away from you, pinch the open ends of the plastic wrap, and continue to pinch and roll until the tenderloin, is completely sealed and resembles a sausage in its casing.

Tie the ends with kitchen twine. This procedure will allow the tenderloin to retain its perfect cylindrical shape while cooking in the sous vide bath.

Using a Cryovac* machine and a commercial-grade vacuum-seal bag, seal the tenderloin following machine directions. Once the sous vide has come to the correct temperature (no less), completely submerge the sealed tenderloin into the bath. Allow to sous vide for 2 to 3 hours.

Note: I sous vide the higher quality cuts of filet (Prime, Wagyu, Kobe) for 2 hours and the lower quality cuts of filet (choice, select) for 3 hours.

Truffled Pomme Purée

1½ pounds potatoes, preferably russet or Yukon Gold
⅓ cup (75 grams) unsalted butter, cubed and chilled
⅓ cup heavy cream (36% M.F.)
½ teaspoon white truffle oil
⅛ teaspoon white pepper
Salt

Peel potatoes and cut into 1-inch cubes. In a stockpot, add potatoes with enough cold water to cover; add salt (1½ tablespoons salt per quart of water) and bring to a boil.
Reduce heat slightly and cook until potatoes are tender when pierced with a fork. When cooked, remove potatoes from heat and strain into a colander*. It may take 2 to 3 minutes to allow all the water to drain.

While the potatoes are draining, warm the cream in a small heavy-bottomed saucepan over low heat. Do not allow to simmer or boil.

Pass the cooked potatoes through a food mill, ricer, or sieve into the original stockpot. Return to low heat and working in small batches, stir in the butter, several cubes at a time, until thoroughly incorporated and creamy. Stir in the warmed cream and truffle oil, and season with pepper and salt to taste.

Reserve covered for service.

Asparagus

Blanching asparagus brightens the color and helps retain vitamins.

24 asparagus spears
2 teaspoons extra virgin olive oil
Salt and pepper
8 parsley sprigs

Prepare ice bath in advance by combining ice and water in a large bowl.

Remove the fibrous ends from asparagus spears and discard; each spear will be about 4½ to 5-inches in length.

In a medium saucepan, bring liberally salted water to a boil (1½ tablespoons salt per quart of water). Add asparagus and blanch 1 minute until they are bright green and still crunchy. Immediately remove from heat, drain, and transfer asparagus to ice bath to stop the cooking process. After 5 minutes, remove asparagus from ice bath, pat dry, and refrigerate for service.
Rinse parsley, pat dry and reserve in refrigerator for plating.

Mushroom Duxelle

8 ounces mixed mushrooms (crimini, button, moral, chanterelle, shitake, etc.), divided
2 teaspoons extra virgin olive oil
3 tablespoons minced shallots
¼ teaspoon salt
¼ teaspoon freshly ground black pepper
2 tablespoons white truffle butter or (2 tablespoons butter and ¼ teaspoon white truffle oil, combined)
1 tablespoon fresh thyme leaves or ¼ teaspoon dried thyme

Finely chop 6 ounces of the mushrooms and slice remaining 2 ounces into larger pieces to use for garnish. Heat a large sauté pan over medium heat. When hot, add olive oil, the 6 ounces finely chopped mushrooms, shallots, and salt and pepper to the pan; cook, stirring frequently, until mushrooms appear dry and are beginning to brown, about 5 to 6 minutes. Stir the truffle butter and thyme into the mixture, remove from heat and reserve for service.

Service

If using the traditional cooking method, remove tenderloin from the refrigerator 2 hours before grilling to allow it to come to room temperature. **Note:** Reheat vegetables while the steak is grilling.

Heat grill to medium-high 400°F to 450°F/205°C to 235°C. Make sure the grill is clean and piping hot. **Note:** Grill will be used for *traditional cooking method* and to finish the sous vide tenderloin.

For the *sous vide method:* once the cooking process is complete, take the vacuum bag from the water bath and remove the tenderloin. Transfer tenderloin to a plate and pat dry; discard the bag and its contents. Sear the whole tenderloin on the grill, 2 to 3 minutes per side and then remove to a cutting board to rest while you plate the dish. **Note:** As a sous vide tenderloin is already cooked, it is grilled only to give additional color, flavor, and texture.

For the *traditional method:* once the whole tenderloin has come to room temperature, sear the meat on the grill until an optimal internal temperature has been achieved depending on preferred doneness. My personal preference is 136°F/58°C (medium-rare). Remove tenderloin from the grill and rest on a cutting board while you plate the dish. Bear in mind that the tenderloin will continue to cook, once removed from the grill, an additional 5°F or 3 to 4°C.

For the Bordelaise Sauce: reheat in covered saucepan over medium-low heat. Check the sauce occasionally and stir to ensure even heating.

For the Pomme Purèe: reheat in covered stockpot over medium-low heat, about 8 to 10 minutes. Check and stir the potatoes every few minutes to ensure even heating.

For the Mushroom Duxelle: while the steak is grilling, add the reserved 2 ounces of raw sliced mushrooms to the duxelle and reheat in a small sauté pan over medium heat, stirring occasionally, about 4 to 5 minutes.

For the Asparagus: while the steak is grilling, heat a small sauté pan over medium heat. When hot, add 2 teaspoons olive oil and asparagus. Lightly sauté spears until they are warmed through and just tender, about 3 to 4 minutes. Remove from heat and season with salt and pepper.

To Plate

Slice the tenderloin into ½ to ¾-inch slices. Using a rectangular serving dish, portion and flatten the Pomme Purée on the center of the plate. Arrange 6 asparagus spears across the Pomme Purée, top with the Mushroom Duxelle and filet.
To finish, garnish with the sliced mushrooms, parsley, and Bordelaise Sauce.

Serves 4

Bordelaise Sauce

1 shallot, finely diced
1 cup dry red wine, preferably *Hahn Pinot Noir*
1 bay leaf
4 to 5 sprigs of thyme
2 cups veal or beef stock
1½ teaspoons unsalted butter
1 tablespoon all-purpose flour
1 tablespoon oyster sauce*
1 tablespoon cognac

In a small heavy-bottomed saucepan combine the shallot, wine, bay leaf, and thyme. Bring to a low boil and reduce contents to ¼ of the original volume to yield ¼ cup.

Add stock and maintaining a low boil, reduce contents by half to yield ⅛ cup; remove from heat.

In a separate small saucepan, melt the butter over moderately low heat. Add the flour and cook, stirring constantly, for 2 minutes. This will allow you to make a roux*. Using a strainer, add the stock mixture in a steady stream to the roux, whisking vigorously to avoid lumps. As you are whisking, continue to cook on low heat at a steady simmer until the desired consistency is achieved. Adjust seasoning with cognac and oyster sauce.

Sous Vide Herb-Encrusted Rack of Lamb

Lamb is an extremely delicate and delicious meat because of its youth. For a beautiful rack of lamb, I like to source grass-fed Australian or New Zealand lamb. Look for a pink to pale red hue with firm white marbling.

Note: An uncooked rack of lamb that has been marinated, seared, and sealed, can be frozen for up to 3 to 4 months.

Advanced Prep (up to 12 hours before service)

Lamb

3 tablespoons extra virgin olive oil
1 tablespoon Worcestershire sauce*
1 teaspoon lamb seasoning from Penzeys Spices* or a mixture of dried oregano, rosemary, cumin, paprika, mint, and ginger
2 x 1½ pound Frenched racks of lamb, each with 8 ribs

In a small bowl, combine olive oil, Worcestershire sauce*, and lamb seasoning.

Remove lamb from packaging, pat dry, and remove excess fat and sinew* from the meat.
Prick rack loins several times with a fork and place in a casserole dish large enough to hold both racks. Rub the olive oil mixture liberally into the loin portion of the racks to marinate. Cover and reserve in refrigerator until service.

To use the *sous vide cooking method*, follow the steps below after the lamb has marinated.
To use the *traditional cooking method,* omit the *sous vide cooking method steps.*

SOUS VIDE METHOD
It is important to seal the juices before sous viding the lamb to achieve optimum flavor.

Heat a large skillet over medium-high heat and sear each side of the racks, including the ends, for 1 minute. Remove the racks from the skillet and allow to rest until cool, about 10 minutes.

Note: While the racks are resting, I use a kitchen torch to scorch the fat cap and bones (not the meat) giving the rib bones and fat cap color as well as additional flavor. This will give the rack a false pretense that it had been roasting in the oven for 20 to 25 minutes.

Preheat sous vide bath to 131°F/55°C. Using a Cryovac* machine and commercial-grade vacuum-seal bags, seal the seared racks following machine directions. Once the sous vide bath has reached the exact temperature (no less), completely submerge the sealed racks into the water bath. Allow to "sous vide" for 2½ hours before service.

Herb Crust

½ cup panko breadcrumbs*
1 packed tablespoon lightly-chopped cilantro
3 packed tablespoons lightly-chopped fresh basil
1 packed tablespoon lightly-chopped fresh parsley
3 packed tablespoons lightly-chopped fresh mint
½ teaspoon salt
¼ teaspoon freshly ground black pepper
4 tablespoons Dijon or truffle mustard
1½ teaspoons liquid honey

To make the crumb mixture: in a food processor, combine the panko*, chopped herbs, salt, and pepper. Pulse until the panko* and herbs are thoroughly combined and resemble green sand; reserve.

To make the honey mustard mixture: in a small bowl, combine the mustard and honey; cover and reserve.

Herb Sauce

1½ cups mint leaves, packed
¾ cup basil, packed
1 tablespoon lemon juice
¾ cup vegetable oil
½ to ¾ teaspoon salt

Prepare ice bath in advance by combining ice and water in a small bowl.

Bring a small saucepan of salted water to a boil (1½ tablespoons salt per quart of water). Add herbs and blanch 15 seconds. Drain and immediately plunge leaves into ice-water bath to stop the cooking process and to retain the vibrant green color. Strain leaves and squeeze as much of the water out as possible. If water remains, wrap the leaves in paper towel, squeeze and wring to remove excess water.

Place herbs and lemon juice in a blender; add oil, just enough to cover the herbs. Turn the blender on medium and blend for 10 seconds. Turn the speed to high and continue to blend. Remove the top from the blender; slowly add the remaining oil in a steady stream and blend for 2 to 3 minutes.

Adjust the seasoning with salt; cover container and reserve in the refrigerator for service. **Note:** Do not heat the sauce, as the enzymes inside the leaves will break down the green chlorophyll, causing the sauce to turn brown.

Polenta

2¾ cups chicken broth
1 small garlic clove, minced
¾ cup quick cooking polenta*
¼ cup unsalted butter
2 tablespoons cream cheese
2 tablespoons minced chives
½ teaspoon salt
⅛ teaspoon white pepper
2 tablespoons all-purpose flour
1½ teaspoons extra virgin olive oil
1 tablespoon butter (2nd amount)

Add broth and garlic to a heavy-bottomed saucepan and bring to a boil over medium-high heat. Reduce heat to low and whisking constantly, gradually pour the polenta* into the liquid. Continue to whisk until smooth and no lumps are visible, cover and stir every 1 to 2 minutes, until cooked and thickened, about 5 minutes. Remove from heat, add butter, cream cheese, and chives and stir to combine. Adjust seasoning with salt and white pepper.

Immediately divide the polenta between two lightly buttered 8 x 8-inch baking pans, level, smooth the top and cool. When cooled to room temperature, cover polenta with plastic wrap and refrigerate until firm.

Before service, remove Polenta* from refrigerator and cut into eight 2½-inch rounds.

Green Beans

Blanching beans brightens the color and helps retain vitamins. For presentation, allow at least 7 or 8 beans per serving.

¾ pound French green beans
2 teaspoons extra virgin olive oil
Salt and pepper

Prepare ice bath in advance by combining ice and water in a large bowl.

Trim the beans at each end so they are uniform and about 2½ to 3 inches in length.

In a medium saucepan, bring liberally salted water to a boil (1½ tablespoons salt per quart of water). Add beans and blanch 1 to 2 minutes until they are bright green and still crunchy. Immediately remove from heat, drain, and transfer beans to ice bath to stop the cooking process. After 5 minutes, remove beans from ice bath, pat dry, and refrigerate.

Ratatouille

1 cup Grilled Vegetables (see Back to Basics page 222)
Salt and pepper
8 ounces micro greens

Cut the grilled vegetables into ½-inch cubes; adjust seasoning with salt and pepper and reserve in refrigerator.

Reserve micro greens in the refrigerator for garnish.

Service

If using the *traditional cooking method*, remove the lamb from refrigerator 2 hours before service to allow it to come to room temperature.

Remove the herb sauce from the fridge and bring to room temperature, do not heat the sauce at is will turn brown.

Note: Reheat the side items to coincide with the chosen cooking method. If using the *traditional cooking method*, sides can be reheated starting 10 minutes before the lamb is removed from oven.

If using *sous vide cooking method*, sides can be reheated 10 minutes before broiling the lamb.

TRADITIONAL COOKING METHOD
Preheat convection oven to 425°F/235°C.

It is important to seal the juices before roasting the lamb to achieve optimum flavor.
Heat a large skillet over medium-high heat. Sear each side of the racks, including the ends, for one minute. Remove the racks from the skillet and allow to rest until cool, about 10 minutes.

Herb Crust: using a pastry brush, coat the surface of the meat with the reserved honey mustard mixture and dredge the coated surface with the crumb mixture, pressing to adhere.

Being careful not to overlap, place the herb-crusted racks fat side up, on a parchment- or Silpat*-lined baking sheet. Roast racks in the oven 20 to 25 minutes to achieve an internal temperature of 125°F to 130°F/51.7°C to 55°C depending on preferred doneness. Bear in mind that the lamb will continue to cook once removed from the oven an additional 5°F or 3 to 4°C.

Remove from oven and rest on a cutting board while you plate the dish.

SOUS VIDE METHOD
Heat the oven broiler on the high setting and place oven rack 6 inches below broiler.

Once the sous vide process is complete, remove vacuum bags from sous vide bath and rest 2 minutes. Remove lamb from vacuum bags to a clean surface, and portion into 8 servings. Form the herb crust: using a pastry brush, coat the surface of the meat with the reserved honey mustard mixture, dredge the honey-coated surface with the herb crumb mixture, pressing the mixture to adhere.

Place the herb-crusted lamb, fat side up, on a parchment- or Silpat*-lined baking sheet. Place baking sheet under the broiler for 2 to 3 minutes until lightly browned and crisp. Remove from oven and rest on a cutting board while you plate the dish.

For the Ratatouille: reheat in a small sauté pan or saucepan over medium heat, stirring occasionally, for 8 to 10 minutes.

For the Polenta*: lightly dust Polenta* rounds with 2 tablespoons all-purpose flour. Heat a sauté pan over medium heat; add 1½ teaspoons extra virgin olive oil and 1 tablespoon of butter to the pan. Sear the dusted Polenta* rounds until golden brown, about 2 minutes per side.

For the Green Beans: heat a medium sauté pan over medium heat. When hot, add 2 teaspoons olive oil and green beans to the pan. Lightly sauté beans until they are warmed through and just tender, about 3 to 4 minutes. Remove from heat and season with salt and pepper.

To Plate

Portion traditional rack of lamb into 8 servings; 2 rib bones per serving.

Place a 3-inch ring mold in the center of a serving plate. Press 2 tablespoons of the ratatouille in the ring mold and carefully remove the mold. Top ratatouille round with Polenta*, Green Beans, and lamb rack. To finish, drizzle the herb sauce around the plate and garnish with micro greens. Repeat the plating for each of the remaining servings.

Serves 8

Sous Vide Pork Tenderloin

Pork is consumed more than any other meat in the world. Many people shy from the consumption of pork due to views regarding sanitation and trichinosis, but if purchased from a reliable source, this delicious protein can remain a part of your balanced diet. I personally purchase Kurobuta pork, which is the Waygu or Kobe of the pork world.

This pedigree breed is a Berkshire pig prized for its delicious flavor and tender meat. It is more expensive than what you will find at your local butcher, but worth every penny.

Note: The cauliflower emulsion and cipollini onions can be prepared in advance and frozen for later use.

Note: The uncooked tenderloin that has been brined, marinated, and sealed can, at this stage (prior to cooking), be frozen for 3 to 4 months.

Advanced Prep (up to 12 hours before service)

Pork Tenderloin

1 to 1½ pounds pork tenderloin
Pork Tenderloin Brine, optional (see Back to Basics page 227)
2 tablespoons extra virgin olive oil
1 tablespoon Worcestershire sauce*
2 teaspoons dried Italian herbs or Penzeys Bavarian Seasoning*
½ teaspoon salt (if the tenderloin has not been brined)

With a sharp knife, remove the silver skin (thin pearlescent membrane of connective tissue that encloses the tenderloin). Removing the silver skin ensures the meat remains tender and does not curl during the cooking process.

Brine the pork tenderloin; this step is optional, but well worth the extra effort.

Create the marinade: in a bowl, whisk together olive oil, Worcestershire sauce*, and seasonings until thoroughly combined. Add ½ teaspoon salt to the marinade only if the tenderloin has not been brined.

Place the brined tenderloin in a large Ziplock bag or container and add the marinade. Seal the bag (or cover the container) and toss the loin to ensure the coats the meat. Refrigerate from 2 hours up to 24 hours. If marinating for longer than 4 hours, turn at least 4 to 5 times during the marinating process. **Note:** A longer marinating time will produce a more flavorful and tender product.

For cooking with *sous vide method,* follow the directions below after the tenderloin has marinated in the refrigerator.
For *traditional cooking method,* omit this step.

SOUS VIDE METHOD
Preheat a sous vide bath to 135°F/57°C or preferred doneness.

Prepare tenderloin for sous vide bath: place two pieces of plastic wrap, overlapping one another and lying flat on a countertop, to make an 18 x 18-inch square.

Remove tenderloin from Ziplock bag, reserving 3 tablespoons of the marinade. Place tenderloin in the center of the plastic wrap square and drizzle with the reserved marinade. Take the bottom seam of the plastic wrap, fold over top of the tenderloin, and pull towards you to cover completely. Now roll the tenderloin in the plastic wrap away from you to create a sausage-like casing. Pinch the open ends of the plastic wrap and continue to pinch and roll upwards until the tenderloin is completely sealed and resembles a sausage in its casing. This allows the tenderloin to retain its perfect cylindrical shape while cooking in the sous vide bath.

Using a Cryovac* machine and commercial-grade vacuum-seal bag, seal the tenderloin following machine directions. Once the sous vide has come to the correct temperature (no less), completely submerge the sealed tenderloin into the bath. Allow to sous vide for 3 to 4 hours.

Cipollini* Onions

Cipollini* onions are absolutely delicious and very versatile. This side dish can be served with numerous dishes; it can be stored in the refrigerator for several days or frozen for later use.

11 ounces cipollini* onions, (about twelve, 1 to 1¼-inch diameter onions)
2 teaspoons extra virgin olive oil
½ cup consommé*
2 teaspoons brown sugar
1½ teaspoons balsamic vinegar
¼ teaspoon salt
⅛ teaspoon ground black pepper
⅛ teaspoon dried Italian herbs

Prepare ice bath in advance by combining ice and water in a large bowl.

Bring a large pot of water to a rolling boil. While the water is coming to a boil, thinly slice off the top and bottom of each onion. Add onions to boiling water and blanch 2 minutes. Drain onions and transfer immediately to the ice bath for 2 minutes. While the onions are still in the ice bath, carefully peel the outer skin from each onion. Remove skinned onions from the ice bath and place on paper towel to dry.

In a medium sauté pan, heat olive oil over medium heat. Add onions to sauté pan and cook until they are browned on all sides, about 5 to 6 minutes. Add consommé* to pan, reduce heat to a low simmer; cover and cook 15 minutes, turning the onions every 5 minutes.

Remove the cover; add the brown sugar, balsamic vinegar, and seasonings to the pan and simmer until sauce is reduced to a glaze consistency and onions are cooked all the way through, about 10 to 15 minutes. **Note:** The size of onion may vary so the cooking times will also vary.

Cauliflower Emulsion

3 cups 1-inch pieces of cauliflower
½ cup ½-inch dice white onion
1 cup vegetable or chicken broth
¼ teaspoon herbes de Provence*
½ teaspoon salt
⅛ teaspoon white pepper
1 to 2 tablespoons Boursin* Herb and Garlic cheese

In a stockpot over high heat, add first 6 ingredients and stir to combine. Bring to a boil, reduce heat to medium-high and cook until vegetables are tender, about 10 minutes. Remove from heat, add the Boursin cheese* and stir to combine.

Using a blender, add the emulsion in batches and purée until smooth. Return emulsion to stockpot; adjust seasoning and reserve for service.

Yields 1½ cups

Green Beans

Blanching beans brightens the color and helps retain vitamins. For presentation, allow at least 7 or 8 beans per serving.

½ pound French green beans
2 teaspoons extra virgin olive oil
Salt and pepper

Prepare ice bath in advance by combining ice and water in a large bowl.

Trim the beans at each end so they are uniform and about 3-inches in length.

In a medium saucepan bring liberally salted water to a boil (1½ tablespoons salt per quart of water). Add beans and blanch 1 to 2 minutes until they are bright green and still crunchy. Immediately remove from heat and transfer beans to an ice bath to stop the cooking process. Remove beans from ice bath after 5 minutes, pat dry and refrigerate.

Campari Tomatoes

2 Campari tomatoes or any ripe 2-inch diameter tomato
¾ teaspoon extra virgin olive oil
Pinch granulated sugar
Pinch salt
2 grinds of cracked black pepper

Preheat oven to 395°F/202°C.

Cut a thin slice from the top and bottom of each tomato so that they stand upright for service, then cut in half widthwise.

Place tomato halves on a parchment- or Silpat*-lined baking sheet so the center of the tomato faces upwards. Evenly drizzle the olive oil over the halves and season with sugar, salt, and cracked pepper.

Bake in oven 8 to 10 minutes until the juices start to release. Remove from oven and reserve for service.

Pancetta Crisp

4 thin slices pancetta*

Preheat oven to 395°F/202°C.

Place pancetta* slices on a parchment or Silpat* lined baking sheet. Bake in oven until crisp and completely dehydrated, about 12 to 15 minutes. Remove from oven and cool completely.

Reserve in a container with a tight fitting lid for service. Do not refrigerate.

Gnocchi

4 large basil leaves, for garnish
8 to 10 ounces gnocchi* (40 to 48 pieces)
1½ tablespoons vegetable oil*
⅛ teaspoon dried Italian herbs
Salt and pepper

Rinse basil leaves, pat dry, and reserve in refrigerator for plating. Reserve remaining ingredients for service.

Service

If using the *traditional cooking method,* remove the tenderloin from refrigerator 2 hours before service to come to room temperature.

Preheat oven to 425°F/235°C.

For the traditional pork tenderloin: heat a large ovenproof skillet or cast iron pan over medium-high heat, add tenderloin, and sear on all sides, 2 to 3 minutes per side. Transfer skillet to the oven and bake 15 minutes or until the internal temperature of the pork registers 140°F/60°C, or preferred doneness. Bear in mind that the

pork will continue to cook once removed from the oven an additional 5°F or 3 to 4°C.

For the Cauliflower Emulsion: heat in a covered saucepan, over medium-low heat, until thoroughly heated. Check occasionally and stir to ensure even heating.

For the Gnocchi: heat a large sauté pan to medium-high heat. Add 1½ tablespoons vegetable oil* and gnocchi to the pan and sauté; stirring and watching carefully so they do not burn for 5 to 7 minutes. When golden brown, remove from heat, and season with Italian herbs, salt, and pepper.

For the Campari Tomatoes: reheat in oven for 5 minutes.

For the Cipollini* Onions: reheat in a small sauté pan over medium-high heat or the microwave.

For the Green Beans: heat a small sauté pan over medium heat. When hot, add the 2 teaspoons olive oil and green beans. Lightly sauté beans until they are warmed through and just tender, about 3 to 4 minutes. Remove from heat and season with salt and pepper.

For the Sous Vide Pork: once the cooking process is complete, remove vacuum bag from the water bath and remove the tenderloin. Discard the bag and its contents; place tenderloin on a cutting board and allow it to rest. Just prior to plating, slice the tenderloin into 4 to 6 ounce portions.

For the Traditional Pork Tenderloin: remove tenderloin from the oven to a cutting board and allow it to rest. Just prior to plating, slice the tenderloin into 4 to 6 ounce portions.

To Plate

Using a ladle, make a pool of the Cauliflower Emulsion in the center of four large serving bowls (pasta bowls) or plates. Arrange 10 to 12 gnocchi on the center of the emulsion, top with 7 or 8 green beans and 1 portion of the pork tenderloin. Beside the tenderloin, plate a Campari Tomato and the Cipollini* Onions.
To finish, garnish with a Pancetta Crisp, basil leaf, and the reduction from the onions.

Serves 4

Sous Vide Ribeye

For this dish, I choose either a 1½-inch or 2-inch thick center cut ribeye or New York strip steak.

Note: I prefer to use USDA Black Angus Prime, Wagyu, or Kobe beef.

Note: The uncooked ribeye that has been marinated and sealed can, at this stage (prior to cooking), be frozen for 3 to 4 months.

Advanced Prep (up to 12 hours before service)

Ribeye Marinade

Balsamic Glaze (see Back to Basics page 213)
4 ribeye or strip loin steaks, 5 to 6 ounces each
2 teaspoons Montreal Steak Seasoning*
1 teaspoon brown sugar
1¾ teaspoons Worcestershire sauce*
3 tablespoons extra virgin olive oil

Prepare the Balsamic Glaze (optional for service).

Pierce the steaks with a fork to tenderize. Rub the steaks liberally with Montreal Steak Seasoning* and sugar and place in a Ziplock bag or container large enough to hold the steak. Pour the Worcestershire sauce* and oil over the steak and rub in liberally. Seal the bag or cover the container and refrigerate for at least 4 hours and up to 2 days. If marinating for longer than 4 hours, turn at least 4 to 5 times during the marinating process.

For the *sous vide cooking method*, follow the directions below after the steak has marinated in the refrigerator.
For the *traditional cooking method*, omit this step.

SOUS VIDE METHOD
Preheat sous vide bath to 131°F/55°C or preferred doneness.
Using a Cryovac* machine and commercial-grade vacuum-seal bags, seal the steaks following machine directions. Ensure that each steak lies flat inside the bag, does not overlap, and does not

touch. Each steak will now have maximum surface area in the water bath.

Once the sous vide bath has reached the exact temperature (no less), completely submerge the sealed steaks into the water bath. Allow to sous vide for 2 to 3 hours.

Spaghetti Squash

2 pounds spaghetti squash
3 tablespoons softened butter
2 tablespoons brown sugar
Salt and pepper

Preheat oven to 400°F/205°C.

Prick the squash skin with a fork, place in a microwave oven and cook on high 2 minutes. Halve the squash lengthwise and remove seeds and membranes. Coat cut side evenly with butter and sprinkle with sugar.

Place squash, cut side up, in a large casserole dish and cover with foil. Bake in preheated oven until fork tender, about 50 to 70 minutes. Remove from oven and cool slightly. Using a fork, remove spaghetti-like strands from the squash to a casserole dish, season with salt and pepper, cover with foil and reserve for service.

Green Beans

Blanching beans brightens the color and helps retain vitamins. For presentation, allow at least 7 or 8 beans per serving.

½ pound French green beans
2 teaspoons extra virgin olive oil
Salt and pepper

Prepare ice bath in advance by combining ice and water in a large bowl. Trim the beans at each end so they are uniform and about 3-inches in length.

In a medium saucepan, bring liberally salted water to a boil (1½ tablespoons salt per quart of water). Add beans and blanch 1 to 2 minutes until they are bright green and still crunchy. Immediately remove from heat, drain, and transfer beans to ice bath to stop the cooking process. After 5 minutes, remove beans from ice bath, pat dry, and refrigerate.

Cherry Tomatoes

6 cherry tomatoes
½ teaspoon extra virgin olive oil
2 pinches granulated sugar
Salt and pepper

Preheat oven to 400°F/205°C.

Cut a thin slice from the top and bottom of each cherry tomato so that they stand upright for service, then cut in half widthwise. Place tomatoes on a baking sheet fitted with a Silpat * or parchment paper so that the center of the halves face up.

Drizzle the top of the tomatoes with olive oil and season with sugar and a pinch of salt and pepper.
Bake in preheated oven 7 to 8 minutes. Remove from oven and cool, leaving the tomatoes in the pan until service.

Horseradish Cream

1 tablespoon prepared horseradish*
¼ cup sour cream or crème fraîche*
2 dashes Worcestershire sauce*
⅛ teaspoon white pepper
⅛ teaspoon salt

Combine all ingredients in a bowl and mix well; reserve in the refrigerator for plating.

Garnish

1 bunch frisée
4 large basil leaves

Rinse frisée and basil leaves, pat dry, and reserve in refrigerator for plating.

Service

If using the *traditional cooking method*, remove the steak from the refrigerator 2 hours before grilling to allow it to come to room temperature.

Preheat oven to 400°F/205°C.

For the spaghetti squash: reheat the covered casserole dish in the oven until the squash is warm and heated through, about 15 to 20 minutes. If desired, remove foil for the final 10 minutes of baking to caramelize.

Preheat grill to medium-high 400°F to 450°F/205°C to 235°C.

Make sure grill is clean and piping hot. **Note:** Grill will be used for *traditional cooking method* and to finish the sous vide steak.

For the sous vide steak: once the cooking process is complete, remove vacuum bag from the water bath and remove the steak from the vacuum bag. Transfer the steak to a plate and pat dry; discard the bag and its contents. Sear the steaks on the grill, 2 minutes per side, and then remove to a cutting board to rest while you plate the dish.

Note: As a sous vide steak is already cooked, it is grilled only to give additional color, flavor, and texture. It is important to have a very hot grill that will give the steak a "charred" effect.

For the traditional steak: once the steak has come to room temperature, sear the steak on the grill until an optimal internal temperature has been achieved depending on preferred doneness. My personal preference is 136°F/58°C (medium-rare). Remove from grill and rest on a cutting board while you plate the dish. Bear in mind that the steak will continue to cook once removed from the grill an additional 5°F or 3 to 4°C.

For the Green Beans: while the steak is grilling, heat a small sauté

To Plate

pan over medium heat. When hot, add 2 teaspoons olive oil and green beans. Lightly sauté beans until they are warmed through and just tender, about 3 to 4 minutes. Remove from heat and season with salt and pepper.

For the Cherry Tomatoes: reheat the tomatoes in the oven 5 to 7 minutes before plating.

Thinly slice the steak. Using a rectangle mold or freeform, portion the Spaghetti Squash in the center of four serving plates (I prefer rectangular plates for this dish) and lightly flatten surface. Arrange 7 to 8 green beans across the spaghetti squash. Fan the steak on top of the beans and garnish with the frisée. To finish, garnish the plate with tomatoes, a dollop of horseradish cream, basil leaf, and the Balsamic Glaze.

Serves 4

Seafood

Butter-Poached Lobster Tail

Lobster is an extremely versatile and delicious crustacean. My preferred preparation method is to butter-poach the delicate tail allowing the meat to remain unbelievably tender and flavorful. Feel free to infuse the butter with optional flavors such as fresh basil, tarragon, curry, or garam masala to create a beautiful twist on this recipe.

This dish is a tribute to an idol of mine whom I have followed throughout my entire career as a chef. I owe a lot of my creativity to the hours I spent studying his delicate refined cuisine. Chef Thomas Keller is an icon, and in my opinion, one of the world's greatest chefs.

Advanced Prep (up to 12 hours before service)

Lobster

6 uncooked lobster tails, shells intact (4 to 6 ounces each)
2 cups (500 grams) Beurre Monté (see Back to the Basics page 215) or unsalted butter
1 teaspoon salt
2 teaspoons fresh lemon juice

Remove meat from the tails; on the underside of the tail, where the cartilage meets the shell, cut a shallow incision lengthwise down each side of the cartilage. Using gloves, carefully discard the cartilage, break open the shell, and remove the meat.

Add the Beurre Monté or butter to a medium bowl and whisk in the salt and lemon juice. Individually mold the lobster tails into perfect rounds and loosely tie with kitchen twine*. In a deep baking dish or loaf pan large enough to hold the tied lobster tails in a single layer with limited space between portions, completely cover with the Beurre Monté. Cover, refrigerate and reserve for service.

Vegetables

1½ cups leek, white part only, cut in ¼-inch rings
2 tablespoons ⅛-inch diced red pepper
2 tablespoons ⅛-inch diced carrot
2 tablespoons ⅛-inch diced celery
2 tablespoons ⅛-inch diced zucchini
2 teaspoon Beurre Monté (see Back to Basics page 215) or butter
1 tablespoon minced parsley

Prepare ice bath in advance by combining ice and water in a large bowl.

In a large saucepan, bring 2 quarts (8 cups) of liberally salted water to a boil (1½ tablespoons salt per quart of water). Add leeks and blanch 2 to 3 minutes. Using a slotted spoon, immediately remove leeks from the boiling water and transfer to the ice bath to stop the cooking process. Remove leeks from ice bath after 5 minutes, pat dry, and refrigerate.

Using the same salted water, repeat blanching process for each remaining vegetable portion. Blanch each vegetable about 1 to 2 minutes until al dente*. Using a slotted spoon, immediately remove from the boiling water and transfer to the ice bath for 5 minutes, pat dry, and refrigerate. The brunoise* (diced) vegetables can be stored together for service. Place the parsley in a small bowl, refrigerate, and reserve for service.

Polenta

1¾ cups + 1 tablespoon chicken or vegetable stock
½ cup quick cooking polenta*
3 tablespoons butter
1½ tablespoons cream cheese
1 tablespoon each minced chives, tarragon, and basil, or a variety of desired herbs
⅛ teaspoon white pepper
Salt

Add stock to a heavy-bottomed saucepan and bring to a boil over medium-high heat. Reduce heat to low and whisking constantly, gradually pour the polenta* into the liquid. Continue to whisk until smooth and no lumps are visible; cover and stir every 1 to 2 minutes, until cooked and thickened, about 5 minutes.

Remove from heat, add the butter, cream cheese, and herbs and stir to thoroughly combine. Adjust seasoning with white pepper and salt to taste.

Add the polenta* to a lightly buttered 8 x 8-inch baking pan; level, smooth the top, and cool on the countertop. When at room temperature, cover the polenta* with plastic wrap and refrigerate until firm.

Before service, remove polenta* from refrigerator and cut into six 2½-inch rounds.

Coral Tuiles

⅔ cup water
¼ cup vegetable oil*
2 tablespoons all-purpose flour
3 drops black food coloring or color of choice
⅓ cup micro greens

In a bowl, combine all ingredients except micro greens and whisk vigorously to emulsify*. Immediately divide the mixture equally into six separate bowls. It is very important to do this while the mixture is combined, as it will separate very quickly.

Heat a dry 5½-inch diameter sauté pan over medium heat. When pan is hot, whisk the batter of one bowl, and pour the entire contents into the pan. Roll the pan with your wrist so that it covers the entire surface as you would with crêpe batter and tap lightly to flatten. Allow the batter to cook and crackle until all water evaporates, the spitting stops, and a crisp tuile remains in the oil. Using the tip of a knife, carefully remove tuile from pan and place on paper towel to absorb the excess oil. Remove remaining oil from the pan with paper towel. Repeat cooking steps with remaining five bowls of batter. Reserve tuiles for plating. **Note:** If preparing in advance, store in an airtight container for up to one day.

Reserve micro greens in the refrigerator for garnish.

Service

If the lobster was reserved in the refrigerator, remove and bring to room temperature at least one hour before service.

Heat oven to 400°F/205°C.

Thirty minutes before service, remove all refrigerated items (except micro greens) and bring to room temperature.

For the Lobster: bake in oven until the internal temperature of the lobster registers 137°F to 140°F/58°C to 60°C, or preferred doneness, about 17 to 25 minutes. The timing will depend on the thickness of the lobster tails.

For the Polenta*: transfer rounds to a parchment- or Silpat*-lined baking sheet and reheat in the oven for 10 to 15 minutes.

For the Vegetables: heat a small sauté pan over medium heat. When hot, add 2 teaspoons Beurre Monté, leeks, and diced vegetables. Lightly sauté until warmed through, about 3 to 4 minutes. Remove from heat, stir in parsley and season with salt and pepper.

To Plate

Using a slotted spoon, remove the lobster from the Beurre Monté and drain on a plate lined with a paper towel. Place a polenta* round in the center of each serving plate. Top with vegetables, lobster, and micro greens. To finish, drizzle the plate with the Beurre Monté and top with the Coral Tuile.

Serves 6

Chilean Sea Bass

Chilean sea bass, also known as Patagonian toothfish, is a species of cod icefish that dwells in the cold deep waters of the Southern Hemisphere. It is prized for its large, snow-white, flaky fillets that are tender, moist, and melt in your mouth. For this recipe it is possible to substitute with any white fish fillet.

Note: I prefer to use coconut cream for this recipe, but it is possible to substitute the cream with coconut milk. The Thai red curry sauce can also be prepared in advance and frozen for later use.

Advanced Prep (up to 12 hours before service)

Chilean Sea Bass

6 Chilean sea bass fillets (4 to 6 ounces each)
½ teaspoon salt
1½ teaspoons vegetable oil*
1 tablespoon clarified butter, Ghee* (see Back to Basics page 219)

Portion the fish fillets, cover and reserve in refrigerator for service. Individually prepare the remaining ingredients and reserve for service.

Thai Red Curry Sauce

13.5 ounce can of coconut cream*or milk
1 teaspoon Thai red curry paste*
¼ cup sweet chili sauce*
½ teaspoon grated fresh ginger
1½ teaspoons soy sauce
1 tablespoon cornstarch
1 tablespoon water

Refrigerate the can of coconut cream* for at least 2 to 3 hours and preferably overnight. Remove can from refrigerator, being careful not to shake the can; scoop out the separated cream, which will have chilled and risen to the surface.
The cream should measure 1 cup; if not, add coconut water from can to equal that amount.

Reserve the remaining coconut water in a separate bowl for the Bok Choy. The sauce that I have made for this dish is mild, but feel free to increase or reduce the amount of Thai Red curry paste* depending on the level of spice preferred.

Combine the coconut cream*, red curry paste, sweet chili sauce*, ginger, and soy sauce in a medium saucepan; cook on medium heat and whisk until sauce is thoroughly combined. This will create a thin sauce, but if you would like a thicker viscosity; combine 1 tablespoon cornstarch with 1 tablespoon water in a small bowl to make a slurry*. Whisk until the cornstarch is completely dissolved; stir the slurry* into the sauce and bring to a low simmer making sure it does not come to a boil. Simmer 5 to 7 minutes to thicken and infuse flavors. Cover and reserve for service.

Coconut Sticky Rice

2 cups sushi rice
13.5 ounce can coconut cream* or milk
1 teaspoon salt
Boiling water
1 tablespoon charnushka*

Sticky rice can be prepared in advance and reheated for service.

Place the rice in a meshed sieve and rinse under cold water for 20 to 30 seconds. I do not rinse until clear in order to maintain more starch for its "sticky" texture.

In a medium saucepan, combine rice, coconut cream*, and salt. Fill the empty coconut cream* can with boiling water and add to saucepan. Bring to a boil, lower heat and simmer for 10 minutes. Turn off heat and set aside (off the burner) for an additional 10 minutes.

Carefully fold in charnushka* seeds and additional salt, if necessary. If preparing in advance; transfer rice to a baking sheet, spreading in a thin layer for rapid cooling. Cover with plastic wrap and reserve on counter for service.

Bok Choy

6 baby bok choy
1 teaspoon sesame oil
⅓ cup reserved coconut water
½ teaspoon soy sauce

Thoroughly rinse the baby bok choy. Remove a thin slice from the base of the bok choy and any unwanted or damaged leaves. Separate the green leaves from the fibrous stems, as they require separate cooking times. Chiffonade* the green leaves and cut the stems into ½-inch square pieces; reserve in two separate bowls. Place damp paper towels over the vegetables, cover with plastic wrap, and refrigerate for service.

Reserve the sesame oil, coconut water, and soy sauce in separate bowls for service.

Keralan Salad

3 tablespoons ⅛-inch diced mango
3 tablespoons thin strips red bell pepper, 1½-inch in length
1½ tablespoons thinly sliced red onion, 1½-inch in length
3 tablespoons fennel, thinly sliced, 1½-inch in length
¾ teaspoon chopped cilantro
Juice of one half a lime
2 tablespoons micro cilantro, for garnish

In a medium bowl, combine mango, red pepper, onion, fennel, and cilantro. Place a damp paper towel over the vegetables, cover with plastic wrap and refrigerate. Reserve the lime juice and micro greens in separate bowls and refrigerate for service.

Service

Preheat oven to 400°F/205°C.

One hour before service, remove sea bass from refrigerator and bring to room temperature.

Thirty minutes before service, remove all remaining refrigerated items (except micro greens) and bring to room temperature.

Transfer cooled sticky rice to a glass bowl for reheating in the microwave. Cover with plastic wrap.

For the fish: season both sides of the sea bass fillets with reserved ½ teaspoon salt. Line a baking sheet with parchment or Silpat*.

Heat a large sauté pan over medium heat. When hot, add 1½ teaspoons vegetable oil* and 1 tablespoon ghee*. Add sea bass to the pan and sear until golden brown, about 2 to 4 minutes per side. Transfer fish to the lined baking sheet and finish cooking in the oven until an optimal internal temperature of 122°F to 125°F/50°C to 52°C, or preferred doneness is achieved, an additional 10 to 15 minutes. Cooking time may vary depending on the thickness of the fillet.

While the sea bass is baking, heat a sauté pan over medium heat. When pan is hot, add 1 teaspoon sesame oil and only bok choy stems. Sauté stems until al dente*, about 5 minutes. Add the coconut water, leaf chiffonade,* and soy sauce to pan and continue to cook until the leaf is wilted and the vegetables are thoroughly cooked, about 2 to 3 minutes.

While the sea bass is in the oven, reheat Thai Red Curry Sauce on stovetop over medium heat. Reheat sticky rice in a microwave oven using moderate heat.

Remove sea bass from the oven for plating.

Toss Keralan Salad with the juice of half a lime.

To Plate

Using a ladle, make a pool of the Thai Red Curry Sauce in the center of a large serving bowl (pasta bowl) or plate. Place a 3-inch ring mold in the center of the sauce and press ⅓ cup coconut rice into the ring mold to create a perfect round that is compact and will not fall apart. Carefully remove the ring mold and top the rice with Bok Choy and Chilean Sea Bass. Garnish with the Keralan Salad and micro cilantro. Repeat the same steps for each of the remaining five servings.

Serves 6

MADE
WITH
LOVE

Eat With Joy

Grilled Atlantic Cod

The addition of Bangkok seasoning brings a subtle Thai flavor to this mild fish, while the bright green beans and brilliant tomatoes add an inimitable pairing and visual appeal. You can substitute the cod with any fish that you enjoy cooking on the grill.

Advanced Prep (up to 12 hours before service)

Cod

½ teaspoon salt
½ teaspoon granulated sugar
4 cod fillets, 1-inch thick (4 to 6 ounces each)
⅓ cup dry white wine, *Hahn Pinot Gris*
¾ cup extra virgin olive oil
½ teaspoon white pepper
¼ teaspoon Bangkok seasoning* or smoked Spanish paprika
⅔ cup packed fresh herbs, coarsely chopped (single or any combination of parsley, dill, fennel frond, cilantro, etc.)

In a small bowl, combine salt and sugar and evenly sprinkle mixture over top and bottom of cod portions to lightly coat in a dry cure. Transfer to a plate and reserve for 2 minutes.

In a small bowl, combine wine, oil, pepper, Bangkok seasoning*, and herbs and whisk to emulsify*.

In a lidded plastic or glass container large enough to hold the fillets in a single layer with limited space between portions, pour herbed oil mixture over cod, turning fish to evenly coat. Reserve and marinate in refrigerator for at least 4 to 6 hours.

Green Beans

Blanching beans brightens the color and helps retain vitamins. For presentation, allow at least 7 or 8 beans per serving.

½ pound French green beans
2 teaspoons extra virgin olive oil
Salt and pepper

Prepare ice bath in advance by combining ice and water in a large bowl.

Trim the beans at each end so they are uniform and about 3 inches in length.

In a medium saucepan, bring liberally salted water to a boil (1½ tablespoons salt per quart of water). Add beans and blanch 1 to 2 minutes until they are bright green and still crunchy. Immediately remove from heat and transfer beans to an ice bath to stop the cooking process. Remove beans from ice bath after 5 minutes, pat dry and refrigerate.

Cherry Tomato Sauce

While the tomato sauce brings color and flavour to this dish, it is equally delicious served with any mild seafood.

12 cherry tomatoes
¼ teaspoon granulated sugar
Pinch of salt
1 tablespoon extra virgin olive oil
1 teaspoon vodka
2 tablespoons butter

Remove a thin slice from top and bottom of each tomato and then cut tomato in half crosswise. Stand tomato halves upright in a saucepan and reserve for service.

In a small bowl, whisk together remaining ingredients and pour over tomatoes. Cover and reserve at room temperature until service.

Soft Scallion Polenta

A staple of northern Italy, polenta* has found its place in many cuisines. The addition of scallions and herbed cheese raises this dish from ordinary to gourmet!

1¾ cups + 1 tablespoon chicken or vegetable stock
½ cup quick cooking polenta*
¼ cup thinly sliced scallion
¼ cup garlic and chive-flavored Boursin* cheese
2 tablespoons butter

Add stock to a small heavy-bottomed saucepan and reserve. Add polenta* to a small bowl and reserve. In a second bowl, combine green onion, Boursin cheese*, and butter; cover and refrigerate.

Zucchini Ribbon Garnish

The colorful arrangement of zucchini ribbons* makes an ideal garnish for many entrées or salads. Be sure to add this recipe to your collection for future use.

1 small green zucchini, rinsed and dried
Micro greens
Fresh herbs of choice, optional

Trim ends from zucchini. Cut lengthwise slices from each side of zucchini to a depth of about ½ inch, making sure you do not include any of the seed area. Using a vegetable peeler, ribbon* the slices in a lengthwise motion; each ribbon* will have one green edge. Place ribbons* in a bowl of ice water and refrigerate.

Clean and dry micro greens and herbs refrigerate for service.

Service

Thirty minutes before service, remove all refrigerated items (except micro greens and herbs) and bring to room temperature.

Preheat grill to medium-high 400°F/205°C to 450°F /235°C. Make sure grill is clean and piping hot.

For the Soft Scallion Polenta*: heat saucepan with stock over medium-high heat and bring to boil. Reduce heat to low and whisking constantly, gradually pour the polenta* into the liquid. Continue to whisk until smooth and no lumps are visible; cover and stir every 1 to 2 minutes. After 5 minutes, add the reserved cheese mixture and whisk until smooth. Keep saucepan covered but continue to stir with a spatula every 1 to 2 minutes until you are ready to plate.

For the Cod: remove cod from marinade, discard all herbs and reserve marinade for basting the cod during cooking. Place cod portions on grill top and cook 4 minutes per side, brushing the marinade on cod as you grill. You will know the fish is cooked when it starts to lightly flake with a fork or has an internal temperature of 122°F/50°C to 125°F/52°C. Remove promptly being careful to keep the portions intact.

For the Green Beans: while cod is grilling, heat a small sauté pan over medium heat. When hot, add the 2 teaspoons olive oil and green beans. Lightly sauté beans until they are warmed through and just tender, about 3 to 4 minutes. Remove from heat and season with salt and pepper.

For the Cherry Tomatoes: while cod is grilling, uncover cherry tomatoes in reserved saucepan and bring to a boil on stovetop. At the boiling point cook for 30 seconds and immediately remove from heat.

For the Zucchini: remove ribbons* from water and place on paper towels to dry. Lightly season with salt. This will allow the zucchini to become more pliable for service.

To Plate

Portion polenta* evenly in the center of four serving plates and lightly flatten the surface. Arrange 7 or 8 green beans on the center of the polenta*. Place cod portion on green beans and spoon the tomatoes and sauce around the polenta*. To finish, arrange zucchini ribbons* on top of cod, and scatter with micro greens and fresh herbs.

Serves 4

Grilled Salmon

This healthy dish is packed with flavor. Feel free to substitute the salmon with other varieties of poached or steamed fish. The salmon presentation shown in the opposite photograph was first brined, then cooked sous vide at 113°F /45°C for 25-30 minutes. The slaw in this recipe is very versatile and I frequently prepare it to serve with tacos, lettuce wraps, or just about any BBQ lunch.

Note: The quinoa, salmon portions, cut vegetables, and Honey Dijonnaise can be prepared in advance, but do not toss the vegetables with the Honey Dijonnaise prior to plating.

2½ cups cooked quinoa (recipe follows)
1½ pounds fresh, antibiotic-free sustainable salmon
1 teaspoon salt
1 teaspoon white pepper
1 tablespoon extra virgin olive oil
½ fennel bulb, thinly sliced
½ cup thinly sliced red or green cabbage
¼ small onion, thinly sliced
2 tablespoons Honey Dijonnaise (see Back to Basics page 223)
12 baby bok choy
2 cups vegetable broth
Micro coriander (cilantro)

Prepare the cooked quinoa; while the quinoa is cooking prepare the remaining ingredients.

Cut salmon into six individual 4 ounce portions; season with salt and pepper and generously brush with olive oil. Reserve salmon on a plate and bring to room temperature.

In a bowl, combine fennel, cabbage, and onion. Add Honey Dijonnaise to vegetables and toss to coat. Cover and reserve in the refrigerator.

Thoroughly rinse the baby bok choy. Remove a thin slice from the base of the bok choy and any damaged or unwanted leaves. Place bok choy in the bottom of a large saucepan and cover with vegetable broth. Bring saucepan to a full boil; at that point, immediately cover the pan and remove it from heat. This will allow the bok choy to steep while you grill the salmon and build your plates. Bring a grill to high heat, add salmon portions and sear 3 to 4 minutes on each side or until an optimal internal temperature of 122°F/50°C to 125°F/52°C, or preferred doneness, is achieved. Cooking time will depend on the thickness of the salmon portions.

To Plate

Divide the quinoa evenly onto each of six serving plates. Place 2 pieces of bok choy, overlapping one another, on top of the quinoa. This will make a flat surface on which to rest each piece of salmon. Place the salmon on the bok choy and top with fennel slaw and micro coriander. Finish with the Honey Dijonnaise and serve.

Serves 6

Cooked Quinoa

½ cup white quinoa
½ cup black or red quinoa
2 cups water
1 teaspoon dried oregano
1 teaspoon dried basil
½ teaspoon celery salt
Salt and pepper

In a medium heavy-bottomed saucepan, combine quinoa, water, and seasonings; stir to combine. Bring to a boil, reduce to a low boil, cover and cook 20 minutes or until quinoa becomes translucent and the germ shows a visible spiral on the exterior of the grains.

Remove from heat and let stand, covered, for 5 minutes or until all the stock is fully absorbed. Fluff with a fork, season with salt and pepper if desired and reserve.

Yields 2½ cups quinoa pilaf

Seared Chilean Sea Bass

The Chilean sea bass in this recipe pairs wonderfully with oven-dried cherry tomatoes. When I have an abundance of tomatoes in the kitchen, I love to take the time to prepare these beautiful semi-dried jewels that will keep in the refrigerator for a month. They can be served to accent numerous dishes and will give the dish an additional visual and flavor appeal. For this recipe it is possible to substitute any white fish fillet of choice.

Advanced Prep (up to 12 hours before service)

Chilean Sea Bass

Oven-Dried Cherry Tomatoes (see Back to Basics page 226)
1½ to 2¼ pounds Chilean sea bass
½ teaspoon salt
¼ teaspoon white pepper
1 tablespoon vegetable oil*

Prepare the Oven-Dried Cherry Tomatoes.

Portion the sea bass into six individual 4- to 6-ounce portions, cover and reserve in refrigerator for service. Ready the remaining ingredients and reserve for service.

Roasted Red Pepper Aioli

It is acceptable to use a 454-gram (16-ounce) commercial jar of roasted peppers for this recipe.

1½ cups roasted, seeded red peppers
1 small garlic clove, minced
1 large egg yolk
¾ teaspoon balsamic vinegar
1¼ teaspoons granulated sugar
¼ teaspoon mixed dry herbs of choice
¼ teaspoon salt
3½ tablespoons vegetable oil*, divided

If using jarred peppers, remove them from the liquid and discard the seeds and skin. In a blender, combine the first 7 ingredients and 1 tablespoon of the vegetable oil*. Blend until thoroughly combined, about 1 to 2 minutes. With the blender running, add the remaining oil in a slow steady stream and continue blending until thoroughly emulsified, about 2 to 3 minutes; reserve for service. **Note:** The roasted red pepper aioli can be prepared in advance and refrigerated for pending use or frozen for later use.

Cauliflower Couscous

6 cups cauliflower, cut in 1½-inch florets
3 tablespoons extra virgin olive oil
½ teaspoon dried Italian herbs
⅛ teaspoon garlic powder
Salt and pepper

In a food processor, pulse the cauliflower just until it looks like coarse meal and resembles traditionally cooked couscous. Remove cauliflower from food processor, place in a Ziplock bag or lidded container, cover tightly and refrigerate for service. Ready the remaining ingredients and reserve for service.

Note: Cauliflower contains sulfurous compounds that are released when cooked, giving off a pungent odor—cauliflower farts.

Asparagus

Blanching asparagus brightens the color and helps retain vitamins.

24 asparagus spears
2 teaspoons extra virgin olive oil
Salt and pepper
½ cup micro greens

Prepare ice bath in advance by combining ice and water in a large bowl.

Trim the fibrous ends from the asparagus spears and then cut the bottom of each spear on an angle. Each asparagus will be around 4½ to 5 inches in length.

Note: Using a vegetable peeler, I like to remove the thin layer of skin from the stems of the asparagus while leaving the head intact. This gives the dish additional visual appeal.

In a medium saucepan, bring salted water to a boil (1½ tablespoons salt per quart of water). Add asparagus and blanch 30 seconds to 2 minutes (depending on the thickness of the asparagus), until bright green and still crunchy. Remove from heat, drain, and transfer spears to ice bath to stop the cooking process. After 5 minutes, remove asparagus from ice bath, pat dry and refrigerate for service.

Reserve micro greens in the refrigerator for garnish.

Service

Preheat oven to 400°F/205°C.

One hour before service, remove sea bass from refrigerator and bring to room temperature.

Thirty minutes before service, remove all remaining refrigerated items (except micro greens) and bring to room temperature.

For the Chilean Sea Bass: season both sides of the portions with reserved ½ teaspoon salt. Prepare a parchment or Silpat*-lined baking sheet.

Heat a large sauté pan over medium heat. When hot, add reserved 1 tablespoon vegetable oil*. Add sea bass to pan and sear until golden brown, about 2 to 4 minutes per side.

Transfer fish to baking sheet, season with reserved ¼ teaspoon white pepper and finish cooking in oven until an optimal internal temperature of 122°F/50°C to 125°F/52°C, or preferred doneness, is achieved, about 10 to 15 minutes. Cooking time may vary depending on the thickness of the fish.

For the Oven-Dried Cherry Tomatoes: I personally serve the tomatoes at room temperature, but if you desire, they may be reheated in the oven on a low temperature setting.

For the Roasted Red Pepper Aioli: heat aioli in a small, covered, heavy-bottomed saucepan over low heat. Check frequently, stirring to ensure even heating and watching that it does not simmer or boil as this will cause the aseparate.

For the Cauliflower Couscous: heat a large sauté pan over medium heat. When hot, add the reserved 3 tablespoons olive oil and sauté the cauliflower, stirring frequently, until cooked through, about 10 to 12 minutes. Season couscous with the reserved herbs, garlic powder, and salt and pepper to taste.

For the Asparagus: heat a small sauté pan over medium heat. When hot, add the reserved 2 teaspoons olive oil and lightly sauté the asparagus until warmed through and just tender, about 3 to 4 minutes. Remove from heat and season with salt and pepper.

To Plate

Place a 3½-inch ring mold in the center of a serving plate. Press the Cauliflower Couscous into the ring mold to create a perfect round that is compact and will not fall apart; remove ring mold. Repeat the same steps for each of the remaining five servings.

Top each round with the fish, four asparagus spears, and the tomatoes. To finish, drizzle with the Red Pepper Aioli, top with micro greens, and dust with freshly cracked pepper. Repeat process for remaining plates.

Serves 6

Seared Scallops

These beautiful pearls of the ocean are one of my favorite varieties of seafood. Scallops are labeled as the number of pieces per pound and I prefer the 10/20 size. I recommend choosing the renowned eco-friendly diver scallops that are marketed as "dry" scallops and are untreated with phosphates. This variety of scallop has a sweet natural taste and they caramelize beautifully.

Note: The asparagus emulsion can be prepared in advance and frozen for later use.

Advanced Prep (up to 12 hours before service)

24 scallops (10/20 size per pound)
Asparagus Emulsion (recipe follows)
¼ cup ⅛-inch diced red pepper
¼ cup ⅛-inch diced yellow pepper
Asparagus tips (reserved from Asparagus Emulsion recipe)
24 medium ravioli (1 pound package, flavor of choice)
2 teaspoon Beurre Monté* (see Back to Basics page 215) or butter
2 teaspoons vegetable oil*
¼ teaspoon dried Italian herbs
Salt and pepper

Remove and discard the abductor muscle from each scallop. Transfer scallops to a paper towel-lined plate, cover, and refrigerate for service.

Prepare Asparagus Emulsion.

Prepare ice bath in advance by combining ice and water in a medium bowl.

In a large saucepan, bring 2 quarts of liberally salted water to a boil (1½ tablespoons salt per quart of water). Add reserved asparagus tips from the asparagus emulsion recipe and blanch 1 to 2 minutes, until al dente*. Using a slotted spoon, immediately remove asparagus from the boiling water and transfer to ice bath to stop the cooking process.
Remove asparagus from ice bath after 5 minutes; pat dry and refrigerate for service.

Using the same blanching water, repeat process for diced peppers.

Garnish

Balsamic Glaze (see Back to Basics page 213)
1 sheet 13 x 8.5-inch filo* pastry
1 teaspoon clarified butter, Ghee* (see Back to Basics page 219)
24 micro basil sprigs

Prepare Balsamic Glaze.

Preheat oven to 375°F/190°C.

Place the filo sheet on a cutting board or countertop, brush ½ of the sheet with ghee* and fold in half to make an 8.5 x 6.5-inch portion; brush remaining ghee* on top. Cut the filo* into 6 right-angled triangles, each with a 1.5-inch base and a height of 6.5 inches.

Transfer triangles to a Silpat*- or parchment-lined baking sheet, season with salt and freshly cracked pepper, and bake in oven until crisp and golden, about 4 to 5 minutes. Remove from oven and cool. If prepared in advance, store in an airtight container.

Reserve micro basil in the refrigerator for garnish.

Service

Thirty minutes before service, remove all refrigerated items (except micro basil) and bring to room temperature.

For the Asparagus Emulsion: heat in a covered saucepan, over medium-low heat, until thoroughly heated. Check occasionally and stir to ensure even heating.

For the Ravioli: in a large stockpot, bring liberally salted water to a boil (1½-tablespoons salt per quart of water). Cook the ravioli as per package instructions, typically about 3 to 4 minutes.

For the Peppers and Asparagus Tips: heat a medium sauté pan over medium heat. When hot, add 2 teaspoons Beurre Monte* and lightly sauté the peppers and asparagus tips until warmed through, about 3 to 4 minutes. Season with Italian herbs, salt, and pepper.

For the Scallops: heat a large sauté pan over medium-high to high heat. When hot, add 2 teaspoons vegetable oil* and sear the scallops, 1 to 1½ minutes per side.

To Plate

Using a rectangular serving dish, plate 4 ravioli overlapping one another in a straight line.

Cover the ravioli with the Asparagus Emulsion and top with the peppers, asparagus tips, and seared scallops. To finish, garnish with the filo* crisp, Balsamic Glaze, and micro basil.

Asparagus Emulsion

340 grams (12 ounces) fresh asparagus
2 teaspoons extra virgin olive oil
⅔ cup ¼-inch diced onion
1 teaspoon herbes de Provence* seasoning
1 cup warm chicken or vegetable broth
¼ teaspoon granulated white sugar
3 tablespoons Boursin cheese*
Salt to taste

Remove the fibrous end from asparagus spears and discard. Remove 1½-inch tips from each asparagus spear and reserve for blanching. Cut the remaining stalk into 1-inch pieces.

Heat olive oil in a saucepan over medium-high heat; add onion and sauté until opaque, about 4 to 5 minutes. Add 1-inch asparagus pieces and sauté until they turn brilliant green, about 1 to 2 minutes.

Add herbs and chicken broth and, maintaining a simmer, cook until asparagus is cooked through, about 5 to 15 minutes, depending on the thickness of the stem. Add the sugar and Boursin cheese* and stir to combine.

Using a blender, purée asparagus mixture until smooth.

Using a mesh sieve, strain purée into a small heavy-bottomed saucepan; cover and reserve for service.

Serves 6

White Wine Miso-Glazed Black Cod

Saltwater black cod or sablefish is native to the deep waters of the Pacific Northwest. In fact, it is neither black nor a member of the cod species as depicted by its name. Highly prized for its buttery flavor and delicate silky texture, it makes it an excellent choice for many seafood dishes. In this recipe I marry the tender white fillets with a *Hahn Pinot Gris* miso glaze.

Note: If using Cilantro Oil (which is optional) for this dish, it must be made at least 24 hours in advance.

Advanced Prep (up to 12 hours before service)

Miso-Glazed Black Cod

Cilantro Oil, optional (see Back to Basics page 218)
⅓ cup white miso paste*
⅔ cup dry white wine, *Hahn Pinot Gris*
1 teaspoon granulated sugar
¼ cup brown sugar
6 black cod fillet portions (4 to 6 ounces each)

Prepare Cilantro Oil.
In a bowl, combine miso paste*, wine, and sugars, and whisk until smooth.

In a plastic or glass container that is large enough to hold the fillets in a single layer and with limited space between the portions, place the cod and pour miso mixture over to completely submerge the fish.

Cover, reserve, and marinate in refrigerator for at least 4 hours and preferably overnight.

Pickled Cucumber and Fennel

¼ cup shaved fennel bulb
1 Persian cucumber
4 tablespoons rice wine vinegar*
½ cup water
1 tablespoon granulated sugar
½ teaspoon cumin seeds
½ teaspoon coriander seeds
1 teaspoon charnushka*

Trim fennel bulb by removing root end and any damaged outside layers.

Using a mandolin*, cut fennel bulb crosswise into very thin slices and cut cucumbers lengthwise into thinly sliced ribbons*.

In a saucepan over medium-low heat, bring vinegar, water, and sugar to a simmer, stirring to dissolve the sugar. When sugar is dissolved, remove from heat, stir in cumin, coriander, and charnushka* and cool completely.

Combine vinegar mixture, cucumber, and fennel slices in a bowl; cover and refrigerate for at least 1 hour and 4 hours maximum.

Coconut Sticky Rice

2 cups sushi rice
13.5 ounce can coconut cream*or milk
1 teaspoon salt
Boiling water
1 tablespoon charnushka*

Coconut Sticky Rice can be prepared in advance and reheated for service.

Place the rice in a fine-meshed sieve and rinse under cold water for 20 to 30 seconds. I do not rinse until clear in order to maintain more starch for its "sticky" texture.

In a medium saucepan, combine rice, coconut cream*, and salt. Fill the empty coconut cream* can with boiling water and add to saucepan. Bring to a boil, lower heat and simmer for 10 minutes. Turn off heat and set aside (off the burner) for an additional 10 minutes.

Carefully fold in charnushka* seeds and additional salt if necessary. If preparing in advance; transfer rice to a baking sheet spreading in a thin layer for rapid cooling. Cover with plastic wrap and reserve on counter for service.

Asian Vegetable Sauté

¼ cup ¼-inch diced red bell pepper
¼ cup ¼-inch diced yellow bell pepper
¼ cup ¼-inch diced orange bell pepper
¼ cup ¼-inch diced zucchini
⅓ cup sugar snap peas, cut on a bias in ⅛-inch slices
24 shelled edamame beans
⅛ cup thinly sliced scallion
1 teaspoon sweet chili sauce*
2 teaspoons tamari sauce*
1 teaspoon sesame oil
½ teaspoon vegetable oil*
2 tablespoons micro herbs

In a bowl, combine all cut vegetables except the scallion. Place a damp paper towel over the vegetables, cover with plastic wrap, and refrigerate. In another small bowl, repeat for the scallion.

Place the remaining ingredients individually in small bowls for later use and reserve the micro greens in refrigerator for service.

Dashi Broth

½ sheet kombu*
2 cups tepid water
2 whole dried shitake mushrooms
1 tablespoon tamari*
2 tablespoons beef consommé*
1½ teaspoons Worcestershire sauce*

Rinse kombu* and pat dry, being careful not to remove the white minerals. In a medium saucepan, soak kombu* and shitake in water for 15 minutes.

Bring saucepan to a simmer and keeping just below boiling point, cook for 15 minutes, skimming* impurities from surface with a slotted spoon. Remove from heat and discard kombu* and shitake. Add tamari*, consommé*, and Worcestershire sauce* to the liquid; stir, cover, and reserve for service.

Service

Thirty minutes before service, remove all refrigerated items (except micro greens) from refrigerator and bring to room temperature.

Preheat oven to 400°F/205°C.

Transfer the cooled sticky rice to a glass bowl so that it can be reheated in the microwave. Cover with plastic wrap.

Remove cod from marinade and place on a Silpat*- or foil-lined baking sheet. When oven has come to proper temperature, place cod in oven and bake 10 minutes.

While cod is baking, reheat Dashi Broth on stovetop over medium heat and microwave rice on moderate heat. This will ensure they heat slowly while the cod is baking.

Heat a sauté pan over medium heat. When pan is hot, add sesame and vegetable oils* to pan. Add sauté vegetables (except scallions), stir and cook, adjusting the temperature so that the vegetables are finished cooking when the cod comes out of the oven. When cooked, remove from heat and stir in the scallions, sweet chili*, and tamari*.

When the 10-minute oven timer is finished, leave the cod in the oven and turn the oven to a high broil.
Broil cod for an additional 2 to 3 minutes or to an internal temperature of 122°F/50°C to 125°F/52°C is reached.

Once complete, remove the cod from oven and using a kitchen torch, torch the top of the cod for additional flavor and visual appeal. **Note:** This step is optional but highly recommended as it adds a unique texture and flavor to the fish.

During this time, remove the pickled vegetables from the liquid and drain on paper towels.

To Plate

Place a 3-inch ring mold in the center of a large-rimmed bowl-style serving dish. Portion and press ⅓ cup Coconut Sticky Rice into the ring mold to create a perfect round that is compact and will not fall apart once the ring has been removed. With the ring still intact, ladle 1 ounce Dashi Broth into the bowl so that it surrounds the rice but never covers it. Carefully remove the ring mold. Repeat the same steps for each of the remaining five servings.

Top each round of rice with Asian Vegetable Sauté and a Miso-Glazed Black Cod portion.

Garnish with Pickled Cucumber and Fennel and micro greens. To finish, drizzle Cilantro Oil around the rice so that it lands in the Dashi Broth for effect and flavor. Repeat for remaining plates.

Serves 6

M/Y PEGASUS IX: BAHAMAS BOUND

Pegasus IX is a yacht that truly depicts her name. Reaching speeds of 28 knots with 4,000 horsepower behind her, she truly spreads her wings and flies across the beautiful turquoise Bahamian waters.

What can I say about the Bahamas other than, "What a gorgeous destination!" I thought that I would miss the Mediterranean, but when you are surrounded by palm trees wafting in the warm breeze, white sand beaches, and pristine turquoise waters, you find yourself in a true paradise with a smile that is impossible to erase.

Chartering in the Bahamas is an enchanting experience for both guests and crew. In the Exumas, Warren weaves *Pegasus IX* through the palm tree-studded islands in a maze of pure white sand and turquoise water. Each day I race to finish my preparations for a chance to swim, snorkel, or dive. With guests and GoPro camera in hand, we disappear beneath the surface to dance and play with dolphins, tropical fish, and coral reefs that are teeming with life.

Desserts

Chocolate Soufflé

Ah, the infamous Chocolate Soufflé! This light and airy melt-in-your-mouth dessert is sure to please every palate. I have baked hundreds of soufflés over the years, and this recipe will always be an all-time favorite.

Note: Always use ½-inch size pieces of chocolate or less to ensure they will fully melt.

For this dish, it is possible to prepare the base up to 12 hours in advance. Just ensure that the base will come to room temperature prior to service.

Crème Anglaise (see Back to Basics page 220)
302 grams (10.67 ounces) dark or bittersweet chocolate, ½-inch pieces or callets* (preferably couverture chocolate*)
1¼ cups whole milk (3.25% M.F.)
2 tablespoons cornstarch
2 egg yolks
3 egg whites
1¼ tablespoons unsalted butter
2½ tablespoons granulated sugar
⅛ teaspoon cream of tartar
5 teaspoons caster sugar*

Prepare the Crème Anglaise.

Place chocolate pieces in a medium-size bowl and reserve.

In a small heavy-bottomed saucepan, whisk together milk and cornstarch to combine. Heat saucepan on medium and stirring constantly, bring milk to a simmer.

Pour the hot milk over the chocolate and stir until smooth; rapidly whisk in egg yolks and reserve on counter. **Note:** This base mixture can be made up to one day in advance.

Preheat oven to 400°F/205°C.

Lightly grease 10 ramekins (½ cup size) with unsalted butter. Coat the ramekins with granulated sugar and shake to remove excess. The sugar will assist the rise of the soufflé and create a nice crunchy exterior.

Using an electric mixer, whip egg whites until frothy; add cream of tartar and beat until soft peaks form. Gradually beat in caster sugar, 1 teaspoon at a time, until sugar is dissolved and stiff glossy peaks form (do not overbeat).

Gently fold the egg whites into the chocolate mixture until thoroughly incorporated and no streaks remain. Ladle chocolate mixture into each ramekin up to the filling line, which is found just below the rim. Bake, resisting any temptation to open oven door, until beautifully puffed and towering high, about 15 to 20 minutes.

Note: I prepare my garnished plates in advance so that the soufflé can be served immediately once removed from the oven.

Garnish

10 edible flowers
1 tablespoon Dutch cocoa powder

To Plate

Place a fork and spoon on the corner of each serving dish. Using a small fine-meshed sieve or tea strainer, dust the fork and spoon with cocoa powder. Gently remove the fork and spoon, being careful not to disturb the cocoa pattern.

Fill ten individual 1- to 2-ounce cream pitchers or small shot glasses with the Crème Anglaise and garnish with an edible flower. Remove soufflés from the oven, plate, and serve immediately, accompanied with the Crème Anglaise pitchers.

Serves 10

Chocolate Torte Round

The chocolate base in this torte recipe is extremely versatile and can become a pedestal for numerous desserts. In this recipe it is used as a chocolate round, but it can also be served alone as a torte with fresh fruit or molded into a delicious truffle treat.

To make Truffles: simply allow the chocolate base to cool and using 2 tablespoon portions, roll into perfect rounds. Dust each round with your choice of Dutch cocoa powder, coconut, crushed candied brittle, or nuts.

Note: Vanilla tuile rounds are optional for this dessert and will give it a wonderful crunch and visual appeal. I create my own stencils using a piece of Silpat* or plastic lid that I measure and cut into the desired shape. For this dessert, I use a ¾ x 9½-inch shape that has been cut out of a 2½ x 11½-inch piece of Silpat*.

Note: The components for this dish can be made well in advance. I also like to prepare the chocolate base, portion it, and freeze up to one month.

Dehydrated Pineapple (see Back to Basics page 221)
Sweet Crumble (see Back to Basics page 228)
Chocolate Sauce (see Back to Basics page 218)
White Chocolate Sauce (see Back to Basics page 229)
Chocolate Ice Cream (recipe follows)
2 tablespoons Vanilla Tuile batter (see Back to Basics page 229)
16 ounces (453.5 grams) dark, bittersweet, or milk chocolate, ½-inch pieces or callets* (preferably couverture chocolate*)
1 cup unsalted butter
6 large eggs
48 to 54 raspberries, depending on size, for garnish
6 small sheets of edible gold leaf (optional garnish)

Prepare the Dehydrated Pineapple, Sweet Crumble, Chocolate Sauce, Chocolate Ice Cream, and Vanilla Tuile recipes in advance and reserve.

Preheat oven to 400°F/205°C.

Coat the inside of an 11 x 7 x 1.5-inch baking pan with butter and dust with flour.

In a small heavy-bottomed saucepan, heat 1 inch of water to simmer. Place the chocolate and butter into a medium heatproof bowl and set over the simmering water; this is the double boiler* method (see Crème Anglaise recipe on page 220 for more description). Stirring frequently, warm the chocolate until just melted. Remove bowl from heat, cool until tepid and reserve.

Using an electric mixer or by hand, whip eggs until they are double in volume. Whisk the eggs into the chocolate mixture until thoroughly combined. Pour batter into the prepared pan and bake in the middle of the oven until cooked through, about 25 to 30 minutes.

Note: To prevent cracking, place a pan of boiling water in the bottom of the oven while it is baking.

Remove torte and water pan from the oven. Using a paring knife, run the tip around the edge of the torte and cool completely, allowing it to set 1 to 2 hours.

Rinse, pat dry, and reserve raspberries in the refrigerator for garnish.

Service

Once the torte has set, using a 2½ to 3-inch ring mold, cut the torte into 6 rounds. The excess torte can be used for another recipe, rolled into truffles, or frozen for later use. Place each round on a cutting board or plate and using a sharp knife, cut a thin strip from the top of each round to level the surface, and attain a ¾-inch height.

Preheat oven to 325°F/163°C.

To make the Vanilla Tuiles: use a Silpat*- or parchment paper-lined baking sheet large enough to fit six of the ¾ x 9½-inch stencils. Position a stencil onto the mat or paper and using an offset spatula, place 1 teaspoon of the batter in the stencil and spread evenly and thoroughly throughout. Carefully remove the stencil and repeat the process to make a total of 6 tuiles.

Bake in the oven until lightly brown around the edges, about 10 to

12 minutes. Immediately remove from the oven and using a clean offset spatula, release the tuiles from the pan and form them around the circumference of each torte round. This process should be done swiftly and completed as close to service as possible. If the tuile is not formed while it is hot then it will become too crisp to mold. If this happens, simply reheat the tuile in the oven until it becomes flexible again, about 1 minute. Remove Bittersweet Chocolate Ice Cream from the freezer to soften. If using a Pacojet*, pacotize the ice cream reserved in the beaker.

To Plate

Place one tuile round in the center of each plate. Top each round with 8 to 9 raspberries, Sweet Crumble, and a quenelle*-like shape of ice cream. Garnish with Dehydrated Pineapple, chocolate sauces, and gold leaf.

Serves 6

Chocolate Ice Cream

1 cup, 6 ounces (170 grams) milk chocolate, ½-inch pieces or callets* (preferably couverture chocolate*)
½ cup heavy cream (36% M.F.)
1½ cups whole milk (3.25% M.F.)
¼ cup Dutch cocoa powder
¼ cup granulated sugar
6 large egg yolks
¼ teaspoon salt

Place chocolate in a medium-size bowl and reserve.

In a medium heavy-bottomed saucepan, whisk together cream, milk, and Dutch cocoa powder to combine. Heat saucepan over medium heat and stirring constantly, bringing mixture to a low boil.

Quickly pour the hot cream mixture over the chocolate and stir until smooth.

In a large bowl, whisk sugar and egg yolks until pale and thick ribbons form, about 3 to 4 minutes. Whisking constantly, gradually add and temper the hot chocolate mixture into the egg yolks until thoroughly incorporated.

Transfer mixture to a heavy-bottomed saucepan and cook, stirring frequently, until mixture thickens, but does not come to simmer, about 4 to 5 minutes. Stir in salt and chill.

Add the chocolate mixture to an ice cream/sorbet maker or Pacojet* cylinder and follow manufacturer's directions.

Coconut Panna Cotta

The panna cottas can be prepared up to 2 days in advance and will need 8 to 12 hours to fully set.

1 13.5 oz. can coconut cream* or milk (preferably cream)
1¼ teaspoons granulated gelatin (see Back to Basics page 222)
⅓ cup maple syrup or agave nectar
Chocolate and White Chocolate Sauces (see Back to Basics pages 218, 229)
8 mint leaves
8 edible flowers
1 tablespoon chopped toasted pine nuts
16 large blueberries, sliced in half
4 strawberries, cut in ¼-inch dice

Add coconut cream to a small heavy-bottomed saucepan; sprinkle gelatin over the cream, whisk, and reserve on the counter for 5 minutes to allow the gelatin to bloom*. When the gelatin has bloomed, heat the saucepan over low heat and whisk gently to dissolve the gelatin. Be careful not to allow the liquid to simmer or boil. When gelatin has completely dissolved, remove saucepan from heat and stir in the maple syrup or agave nectar.

Divide the cream evenly between eight individual serving dishes. To create a nice visual effect, I like to offset the panna cotta in their serving dishes, setting the dishes on an angle in an egg carton or muffin tin and using paper towel or aluminum foil to stabilize the bases. Refrigerate serving dishes for at least 8 hours or until completely set.

Prepare the Chocolate and White Chocolate Sauces. Rinse the mint leaves and edible flowers; pat dry and reserve. Prepare remaining ingredients for garnish.

Remove the serving dishes from the refrigerator and garnish each with chopped pine nuts, fruit, mint, and edible flowers.

Garnish plates with the chocolate sauces.

Note: To learn more about how to use gelatin, see Back to Basics.

Serves 8

Dark Chocolate Mousse

For this dessert I use Russian tale silicone molds. Feel free to use a mold of your choice, or for a simplified plating option, divide the mousse between eight individual serving dishes, cover, and chill until set, at least 2 hours. This serving option will omit the need to freeze the mousse as there will be no need to remove them from the silicone mold. Bear in mind that this option will not give you the same exquisite dessert presentation.

I also utilize smoking cloche domes (purchased on Amazon) to cover the dessert so that it is served under a blanket of cold smoke. The amazing visual appeal and light smoky flavor will "Wow!" your guests and friends.

Note: The components for this dish can be made well in advance. The chocolate mousse mold will need to be prepared at least 24 hours and up to 1 month in advance.

4 ounces (113.5 grams) dark chocolate, ½-inch pieces or callets* (preferably couverture chocolate*)
7 tablespoons (3½ ounces) unsalted butter
2 large eggs, separated
1 tablespoon caster sugar*
¾ cup heavy cream (36% M.F.)
Pinch of salt
8 Ferrero Rocher* chocolates
Chocolate Crumble (see Back to Basics page 217)
White Chocolate Sauce (see Back to Basics page 229)
Chocolate Sauce (see Back to Basics page 218)
Raspberry Coulis (see Back to Basics page 227)
8 raspberries
8 small mint leaves

In a small heavy-bottomed saucepan, heat 1 inch of water to simmer. Place the chocolate and butter in a medium heatproof bowl and set over the simmering water; this is the double boiler* method (see Crème Anglaise recipe in Back to Basics for more description). Stirring frequently, warm the chocolate until just melted. Remove bowl from heat, cool until tepid and reserve.

Using an electric mixer, whip egg whites on medium-high speed until soft peaks form, about 1 to 2 minutes. Gradually beat in caster sugar, 1 teaspoon at a time, until sugar is dissolved and stiff glossy peaks form, about 2 to 3 minutes (do not overbeat). Transfer the whites to another bowl and reserve.

In a bowl large enough to hold all ingredients, thoroughly combine the egg yolks and salt. Using a rubber spatula, stir the chocolate mixture into the egg yolks. Gently fold the whipped egg whites and then the whipped cream into the chocolate until no streaks remain.

Thoroughly clean the original mixer bowl and whisk. Using the mixer, beat the whipping cream until soft peaks form.

For this recipe, the mousse yields enough for eight ⅜ cup capacity silicone molds or serving dishes.

Using a silicone mold of choice, fill each mold with chocolate mousse. With an offset spatula, press firmly down on the mousse to eliminate air pockets and ensure all sides of the mold are completely covered. Indent a 1½-inch deep hole in the center of the mousse and place a Ferrero Rocher* chocolate in the hole; press down firmly to submerge the Rocher in the mousse. Add additional mousse to cover the Rocher and flatten the base of the mold; cover with plastic wrap and freeze overnight or until completely solid.

Note: The individual desserts will need to defrost in the refrigerator 3 to 4 hours prior to service.

Prepare the Chocolate Crumble, White Chocolate and Chocolate Sauces, and Raspberry Coulis.

Rinse raspberries and mint leaves; pat dry and reserve in the refrigerator.

Service

Take the mousse from the freezer and immediately remove them from the silicone molds. Place mousse in refrigerator to completely defrost, about 3 to 4 hours.

Cut ⅓ off the top of each raspberry so you have a visible hole throughout each piece of fruit. Tuck one mint leaf into each hole so that half of the mint leaf is exposed and standing tall.

Optional: Prepare a hand smoker with cherrywood chips and have ready for plating.

To Plate

On each of eight serving plates, decorate the rims with dots of the White Chocolate and Chocolate Sauces and Raspberry Coulis. In the center of each plate, build a small mound of Chocolate Crumble, flatten crumble and top with the chocolate mousse. Garnish with a halved raspberry and mint leaf.

If smoking, cover each dessert with a dome and gently fill domes with cherrywood smoke. Serve immediately.

Serves 8

Frozen Bittersweet Chocolate Tart

This tart is very easy to prepare and ideal to have readily available in the freezer for a quick dessert. I use a rectangular loaf pan for this recipe, but feel free to use pans of various shapes and sizes. It is also delicious served with fresh fruit, a dollop of whipped cream, or a light dusting of powdered sugar.

I will sometimes substitute 4 to 8 ounces of the bittersweet chocolate for milk chocolate to create a sweeter version of this decadent dessert. **Note:** Always use ½-inch size pieces or less of chocolate to ensure they will melt in full.

Note: The components for this dish can be made well in advance. The chocolate tart will need to be prepared at least 24 hours and up to 1 month in advance.

Dehydrated Pineapple (see Back to Basics page 221)
Chocolate Crumble (see Back to Basics page 217)
Chocolate Sauce (see Back to Basics page 218)
Bittersweet Chocolate Ice Cream (recipe follows)
75 grams (2.65 ounces) Biscoff* or other commercial chocolate cookies
2 tablespoons (1 ounce) melted unsalted butter
225 grams (8 ounces) bittersweet chocolate, ½-inch pieces or callets*
⅛ cup chopped, lightly salted almonds or nut of choice
½ cup heavy cream (36% M.F.)

Preheat oven to 350°F/177°C.

Prepare the Dehydrated Pineapple, Chocolate Crumble, Chocolate Sauce, and Bittersweet Chocolate Ice Cream recipes in advance and reserve.

Spray a 3½ x 7½-inch rectangular loaf pan with nonstick cooking spray.

Line the pan with two strips of parchment: a lengthwise strip 3¼ x 15-inch and a width strip 7¼ x 15-inch long. Spray nonstick cooking spray between the parchment layers; firmly press the strips to adhere, overlapping into place and creasing the edges to remain intact. Spray an additional layer of cooking spray into the pan once the inserts are complete.

In a food processor, process cookies until finely ground. In a medium bowl, combine ground cookies and melted butter until the mixture resembles wet sand. Firmly press the mixture into the bottom of the loaf pan to create a flat, even surface. Bake 10 minutes; remove from oven and cool.

Place the bittersweet chocolate in a medium-size bowl.

In a heavy-bottomed saucepan, heat cream over medium heat; insert an instant read thermometer and bring to 158°F/70°C. Pour the warmed cream over the bittersweet chocolate and stir until smooth. Stir in the nuts and carefully pour the mixture into the cooled tart base. Keeping the pan flat, shake, tap, and lightly hit on the counter to flatten and remove any air bubbles that rise to the surface.

Allow tart to cool completely; cover and freeze for at least 24 hours prior to service.

Garnish

6 mint sprigs
18 raspberries
6 macaroons, homemade or store-bought

Rinse, pat dry, and reserve mint sprigs and raspberries in the refrigerator for garnish.

Service

Remove the ice cream from the freezer to soften. If using a Paco-jet*, pacotize the ice cream following manufacturer's instructions.

Fill a tall, heavy-bottomed glass with hot water. Set a thin paring knife and an 8-inch utility or chef knife in the water to warm.

Remove the chocolate tart from freezer and run the tip of the warmed paring knife around the edge of the tart. Gently remove tart from the pan with the assistance of the overlapping parchment paper. If difficult to remove, apply gentle heat to the bottom of the pan with a kitchen torch until it has released.

Place the tart on a cutting board. Dry the warmed utility or chef knife and use it to cut the tart into six equal portions.

To Plate

Using a pastry brush, "paint" the chocolate sauce onto the base of 6 individual plates. Place 1 portion of the tart on each plate, top with 3 raspberries, a macaroon, and a mint sprig. Build a small mound of the Chocolate Crumble to the right of the tart, lightly flatten, and top with a quenelle*-shaped portion of chocolate ice cream. The crumble will absorb the melted ice cream and keep the quenelle* static on the plate. Garnish with Dehydrated Pineapple and additional chocolate "dots."

Serves 6

Bittersweet Chocolate Ice Cream

170 grams (6 ounces, 1 cup) bittersweet chocolate, ½-inch pieces or callets* (preferably couverture chocolate*)
½ cup heavy cream (36% M.F.)
1½ cups whole milk (3.25% M.F.)
¼ cup Dutch cocoa powder
¼ cup granulated sugar
6 large egg yolks
¼ teaspoon salt

Place chocolate in a medium-size bowl and reserve.

In a medium heavy-bottomed saucepan, whisk together cream, milk, and cocoa to combine. Stirring constantly, heat saucepan on medium and bring mixture to a low boil. Immediately pour the hot milk over the chocolate and stir until smooth. Reserve saucepan for later use.

In a large bowl, whisk together sugar, egg yolks, and salt until pale and thick ribbons form, about 3 to 4 minutes. Whisking constantly, gradually temper the hot chocolate mixture into the egg yolk mixture until thoroughly incorporated.

Transfer mixture to original saucepan and cook, over medium-low heat, stirring frequently, until mixture thickens, but does not come to a simmer, about 4 to 5 minutes. Remove from heat and allow to cool completely, refrigerate for 1 to 2 hours until thoroughly chilled.

Add the chilled mixture to an ice cream/sorbet maker or Pacojet* cylinder and follow manufacturer's directions to make the ice cream.

Yields 3¼ cups ice cream base

Hahn GSM Poached Pear

For this dessert I prefer to use Bosc pears. The Bosc's firm flesh allows this variety of pear to retain a perfect shape once poached and the crisp, mild sweetness of the fruit is a perfect canvas for the mélange of flavors that the poaching liquid provides. I have poached pears hundreds of times and by far my favorite infusion is with *Hahn GSM* wine, but any red wine can be used.

The garnish for this dessert, crumiel, is honey in its crystallized form. The powdered honey is very diverse and can be used to enhance and add honey flavor to a variety of dishes. I purchase this product online from Modernist Pantry.

Advanced Prep (up to 6 hours before service)

6 candied pear slices (see Back to Basics page 216)
Mascarpone Whip (recipe follows)
Chocolate Sauce (see Back to Basics page 218)
1 bottle full-bodied red wine, preferably *Hahn GSM*
½ cup granulated sugar
½ cup orange juice
Zest from 1 orange
8 whole cloves
2 cinnamon sticks
2 star anise*
4 allspice berries
6 medium Bosc or D'Anjou pears
¼ cup granulated sugar (2nd amount)
½ cup chocolate torte base (page 182) or 6 store-bought chocolate truffles, 1-inch diameter
¼ cup texturas crumiel*
6 mint sprigs

Prepare the candied pear slices, Mascarpone Whip, and Chocolate Sauce and reserve for service.

Make your poaching liquid by combining the next 8 ingredients (wine through allspice), in a medium heavy-bottomed saucepan. Cover the saucepan, bring to a boil and then immediately reduce to simmer and cook for 3 to 4 minutes to allow flavors to infuse. Remove saucepan from heat and reserve.

Cut a ¾- to 1-inch slice from the base of each pear, and peel the skin. Using a small spoon or melon baller*, make a hole in the base of the pear large enough to remove the seeds and later stuff with a 1-inch round chocolate truffle.

One by one, place the pears in a large bowl of water once the skin has been removed to prevent browning (oxidation).

Return the reserved poaching liquid to heat and bring to a low simmer. Remove pears from water and gently add to the poaching liquid. Place two pieces of paper towel on the surface to keep the pears submerged. Poach on medium-low setting (barely simmering) for 12 to 15 minutes and rotate the pears every 5 minutes to ensure even poaching. The pears are complete when al dente*, or when pierced with a knife there is still some resistance.

Remove the paper towel, gently squeeze out excess liquid and reserve the towel. Using a slotted spoon, carefully remove the pears to a plate and cover with the reserved paper towel. Measure 1 cup of poaching liquid and transfer to a small sauté pan. Keep the remaining poaching liquid in the saucepan for later use.

Prepare the GSM Wine Reduction: heat the small sauté pan with poaching liquid to a low-simmer and gently whisk in ¼ cup sugar. Keeping the liquid at a simmer, reduce to a syrup consistency, about 10 to 12 minutes. Remove from heat and reserve for plating.

Prepare the Chocolate Truffles: if using the chocolate torte base, roll 6 chocolate truffles, 1-inch in diameter, cover and reserve on countertop for service. If using store-bought truffles, ensure that the size will fit into the base of each pear, cover and reserve on countertop for service.

Service

Preheat oven to 300°F/163°C.

Reheat the poaching liquid to just below a simmer. Submerge the pears in the liquid for 4 to 5 minutes to reheat.

Using a mesh strainer, "dust" the crumiel powder evenly over a Silpat*- or parchment-lined baking sheet to form a 12 x 8-inch rectangle. Bake the crumiel in the oven 4 minutes. Once complete, remove from oven and using gloves, pull melted crumiel into 6 long "handkerchiefs" for garnish.

To Plate

Form the Mascarpone Whip into quenelle* shapes and plate on each of six serving plates. Remove the pears from the poaching liquid and transfer to a paper towel-lined plate to absorb excess liquid. Stuff the base of each pear with a chocolate truffle and immediately plate next to the mascarpone.

To finish, garnish each pear with a crumiel handkerchief, mint sprig, candied pear slice, chocolate sauce, and red wine reduction.

Serves 6

Mascarpone Whip

6 tablespoons mascarpone cheese
1 teaspoon sifted* powdered sugar*

In a small bowl, thoroughly combine the mascarpone and sugar; reserve for plating.

Healthy Dried Fruit Truffles

This vegan truffle is a healthy alternative to the decadent chocolate truffle. The recipe can be modified and used as a torte, cake, entremet base, or shaped into a bar for a healthy snack; the possibilities are endless.

Note: The healthy dried fruit base can be prepared in advance and frozen for up to 3-4 months.

¼ cup Marcona almonds
¾ cup dates
¾ cup dried figs
½ cup prunes
¼ cup + 1 tablespoon Dutch cocoa powder
Ground pistachio nuts
Dutch cocoa powder for dusting (2nd amount)
Shredded coconut

In a food processor, pulse the almonds until they resemble coarse sand, making sure they are not ground to a fine paste. Remove from the food processer and reserve in a bowl.

Add the dates, figs, and prunes to the food processor; pulse until combined and no large chunks remain.

Add the cocoa powder and reserved ground almonds to the dried fruit mixture and process until combined and soft dough forms. Place mixture in a bowl and chill in the refrigerator for 2 hours. This will allow the mixture to cool and firm, making it easier to roll the truffles.

Using an ice cream scoop or large spoon, scoop out 18 uniform portions of the mixture and roll into perfectly round balls. Transfer balls to a Silpat*- or parchment-lined baking tray and reserve in the refrigerator for service.

Just before service, place the pistachios, cocoa, and coconut in three separate bowls. Roll 6 of the truffles in the ground pistachio, 6 in the cocoa, and 6 in the coconut, garnish and serve.

Serves 6

New York Cheesecake

It is ideal for the cheesecake to be made a day in advance so that it has time to set in the refrigerator. When using the ban marie* cooking method, the hot water buffers the direct heat during the cooking process, creating a moist environment that evenly bakes the sides to the center of the dessert. This method produces an evenly cooked, light, moist, airy dessert.

I have added a list of different garnishes that can be used to accentuate this luscious dessert. Feel free to use your imagination and create the perfect cake you have always dreamed of.

Note: The garnishes and mirror glaze for this dish can be made well in advance. The cheesecake will need to be prepared at least 4 hours up to 24 hours in advance and can then be frozen for up to 1 month.

Note: For the optional mirror glaze, you will need an additional 12 hours to freeze the cake for glazing.

Candied Star Fruit Slices (see Back to Basics page 216)
Dehydrated Pineapple (see Back to Basics page 221)
Chocolate Garnish (see Back to Basics page 217)
150 grams (5.25 ounces) dry cookies (graham, vanilla, gingersnaps, etc.)
½ cup ground almonds
½ cup melted butter
1 tablespoon granulated sugar
1 vanilla bean
1 cup granulated sugar (2nd amount)
4 (8 ounce) packages cream cheese at room temperature
¼ cup cornstarch
2 large eggs
¾ cup heavy cream (36% M.F.)
3 teaspoons lemon juice
1½ cups sour cream
¼ cup granulated sugar (3rd amount)
Mirror Glaze (recipe follows), optional

Prepare the Candied Star Fruit Slices, Dehydrated Pineapple, and Chocolate Garnish in advance and reserve. **Note:** As it is optional to serve the cheesecake with the above garnishes, feel free to simplify the dessert and serve with fresh fruit only.

Preheat oven to 350°F/177°C.

Prepare a 9-inch springform pan; spray with nonstick cooking spray and line the base and sides with parchment paper. Firmly press the parchment paper to adhere and spray an additional layer of the nonstick spray over it.

Wrap the bottom and sides of the exterior of the pan in multiple layers of wide, heavy-duty aluminum foil to form a tight shell or barrier for the ban marie*.
It is ideal to use 3 to 4 layers of 16-inch wide aluminum foil to prevent water from touching the pan.

In a food processor, grind the cookies and almonds until a fine crumb is achieved. In a medium bowl, combine ground cookie mixture, melted butter, and 1 tablespoon sugar until it resembles wet sand. Press the mixture into the bottom of the springform pan so that it is compact and has a flat even surface. Bake for 10 minutes; remove from oven and cool.

To remove seeds from the vanilla bean, run the tip of a pairing knife lengthwise down the center of the bean to expose the seeds inside and split the bean into two pieces. Place the halves, skin side down on a cutting board. Using the dull edge of a knife, run the knife down the center of each pod to remove the seeds. In a small bowl, use your fingertips to thoroughly combine the vanilla seeds and ⅓ cup sugar (2nd amount) so that no clumps remain.

Note: The empty vanilla pods can be utilized to infuse various liquids or added to a jar of sugar to create vanilla-scented sugar.

Using an electric mixer fitted with the paddle attachment, beat one package of the cream cheese, ⅓ cup vanilla sugar, and cornstarch on low until creamy, about 3 minutes. During the mixing process, scrape the sides of the bowl several times to ensure even distribution. Blend in the remaining 2 packages of cream cheese.

Increase the mixer speed to medium and beat in the remaining ⅔ cup sugar (2nd amount) and eggs, one at a time, until thoroughly incorporated. Add the cream and lemon juice to the batter and mix until just combined, being careful not to overbeat. The filling will appear light, creamy, and airy. Gently spoon the mixture over the cooled cheesecake base.

Tightly cover the top of the springform pan with one sheet of aluminum foil and place the pan in a high-sided baking pan that is large enough to hold both the springform pan and water for the ban marie*. I prefer to place the pan into the oven and slowly add the hot water until it reaches ½ to ⅔ of the way up the sides of the springform pan. Bake until the center barely jiggles, about 1¼ to 1½ hours. If the cake still feels soft around the edge, let it bake for an additional 10 to 15 minutes.
While the cheesecake is cooking, prepare the sour cream topping. In a medium bowl, thoroughly combine the sour cream and ¼ cup sugar (3rd amount).

Once the cheesecake has finished cooking, remove it from the water bath and discard the aluminum foil cover (not the bottom). Pour the sour cream mixture over the top, smooth with an offset spatula and lightly tap on the counter to level the sour cream mixture. Return cheesecake to the oven and bake an additional 10 minutes.

Remove from the oven, discard aluminum foil bottom, and transfer to a baking rack. Run a paring knife around the edge to release the sides from the pan and cool 2 hours. Once completely cool; cover and refrigerate for at least 4 hours to overnight.

Proceed to service if you are omitting the Mirror Glaze.

MIRROR GLAZE METHOD:
For a mirror-glazed cheesecake: once the cheesecake has set in the refrigerator, remove from the springform pan, smooth the edges with a palate knife, and transfer to the freezer for at least 12 hours prior to glazing. The cake must be completely frozen prior to pouring the glaze. **Note:** Smooth the top and sides as much as possible as any imperfection will show through the finished glaze.

Prepare the Mirror Glaze and glaze 6 to 8 hours prior to service. This will give the cheesecake time to defrost thoroughly and set.

Mirror Glaze

15 grams (4½ teaspoons) granulated gelatin
⅓ cup cold water
⅓ cup + 1½ tablespoons water (2nd amount)
1 cup granulated sugar
⅔ cup glucose syrup or corn syrup
½ cup sweetened condensed milk
1¼ cups white chocolate, ½-inch pieces or callets* (preferably couverture chocolate*)
½ to 1 teaspoon desired food coloring

In a small bowl, whisk the gelatin into the cold water and allow to bloom* for 5 minutes.

In a medium heavy-bottomed saucepan, whisk together ⅓ cup + 1½ tablespoons water, sugar, and glucose to combine. Heat saucepan on medium and stirring constantly, bring mixture to a simmer until sugar is dissolved, about 3 to 4 minutes. Remove from heat and whisk in the gelatin until thoroughly incorporated. Add the condensed milk and chocolate, and stir until the chocolate has completely melted. Using an immersion blender, emulsify the mixture for 1 minute, strain and cool.

To Glaze: once the mirror glaze has dropped in temperature to 32°C/90°F to 34°C/93°F; add desired color for the finished glaze, stir and strain into a suitable pitcher for pouring. Cover a baking sheet with plastic wrap and fit with a baking rack to catch residual glaze. Have a straight cake spatula on hand to flatten and perfect the glaze.

Remove the cheesecake from the freezer and set on a baking rack. Pour the glaze over the cheesecake in a circular motion ensuring that the sides have been completed covered. Using the spatula, hold it perfectly level to the top of the cake and swipe, just barely touching the top, to flatten and remove residual glaze. Allow glaze to set for a few minutes, and then, using a paring knife, cut the glaze that has dripped from the bottom of the cake. Transfer cake to a serving plate and refrigerate for 6 to 8 hours prior to service. This will give the cheesecake time to defrost thoroughly and set.

Omit the service step of this recipe if using the Mirror Glaze.

Service

I prefer to portion the cheesecake into perfect rounds. Using a 2.5-inch ring mold, cut the cheesecake into the desired number of portions.

To Plate

It is possible to plate this dessert in a variety of ways. Use the photographs provided as a guide, or allow your artistic creativity to take hold and create something wonderful, extravagant, and worthy of a photo shoot!

Yields a 9-inch cheesecake

Peach Mousse Entremet

For this dessert, I use a silicone mold with a 6 to 7 tablespoon capacity. Feel free to use a mold of your choice, or for a simplified serving option, divide the prepared mousse between eight individual serving dishes, chill, and serve.

To shape the Vanilla Tuiles, I create my own stencils using a piece of Silpat* or plastic lid that I measure and cut into the desired shape.

Note: The peach mousse molds will need to be prepared at least 24 hours and up to 1 month in advance.

Peach Ice Cream (recipe follows)
Vanilla Cake (recipe follows)
Sweet Crumble (see Back to Basics page 228)
White Chocolate Sauce (see Back to Basics page 229)
Raspberry Coulis (see Back to Basics page 227)
3 tablespoons + 1 teaspoon Vanilla Tuile batter (see Back to Basics 229)
⅞ teaspoon chopped pistachio or pine nuts
¼ cup water
1 tablespoon gelatin
1½ cups peeled peach cut in ½-inch dice
1 teaspoon lemon juice
1 cup heavy cream (36% M.F.)
1½ tablespoons granulated sugar
3 tablespoons + 1 teaspoon peach jam
20 raspberries
12 edible flowers or mint sprigs
3 semi-firm peaches

Prepare the Peach Ice Cream, Vanilla Cake, Sweet Crumble, White Chocolate Sauce, Raspberry Coulis, and Vanilla Tuile batter.

For the Vanilla Tuile: preheat oven to 325°F/163°C.
To make the tuiles: place a leaf stencil on a Silpat*-or parchment paper-lined baking sheet. Using an offset spatula, place 1 teaspoon of the batter into the stencil and spread evenly and thoroughly throughout. Carefully remove the stencil and repeat for a total of 10 tuiles; sprinkle the tuiles evenly with the chopped nuts.

Bake in preheated oven until lightly brown around the edges, about 8 to 10 minutes. Immediately remove baking sheet from oven and allow to cool. Using a clean offset spatula, remove tuiles from baking sheet and reserve in a lidded airtight container.
To prepare the Mousse: add ¼ cup water to a small heavy-bottomed saucepan; whisk the gelatin into the water and allow to bloom* for 5 minutes.

Using a blender, purée the peaches and lemon juice on the highest setting until smooth. Pass the mixture through a sieve and then return it to the blender.

Heat the bloomed gelatin saucepan over low heat. Whisk constantly to completely dissolve the gelatin and be careful not to let it simmer or boil. Remove saucepan from heat; turn the blender on and add gelatin to the peach purée in a steady stream until thoroughly combined.

Transfer the peach purée to a bowl and chill in the refrigerator until mixture begins to thicken, about 1 hour.

With an electric mixer, whip the cream, adding sugar 1 teaspoon at a time, until stiff peaks form. Fold the whipped cream into the peach purée until thoroughly combined and no streaks remain.

Using a silicone mold of choice, fill each mold with the peach mousse. As you fill the molds, press firmly down and around all sides to completely cover and eliminate any air pockets. Leave a 1–inch deep round hole in the center of each mold to insert the Vanilla Cake round. This recipe will fill 10 silicone molds each with a 4½-tablespoon capacity.

Spread 1 teaspoon peach jam onto each of the cake rounds. Insert the cake rounds, jam side down, into the center of each mousse; push down to submerge all sides. Remove any excess mousse with an offset spatula, cover with plastic wrap and freeze for service. Allow to freeze overnight or until completely solid.

Note: The individual desserts will need to defrost in the refrigerator 4 to 5 hours prior to service.

Rinse, pat dry, and reserve raspberries, flowers, or mint sprigs in the refrigerator for garnish.

Service

Remove the peach mousse from the freezer and immediately remove from each mold; place on small individual plates, and refrigerate for 4 to 5 hours to defrost completely.

Thinly slice the 3 semi-firm peaches and form into 10 peach flowers.

Remove the ice cream from the freezer to soften. If using a Pacojet*, pacotize the ice cream reserved in the beaker for plating.

To Plate

Decorate the rim of the each serving plate with the White Chocolate Sauce and Raspberry Coulis. Transfer the peach mousse to the right of the center of each plate and top the mousse with a peach flower. Build a small mound of the crumble next to the mousse and lightly flatten.

Mold the ice cream into a quenelle* shape and lay on the flattened crumble mound. This will absorb the melted ice cream and keep the quenelle* static on the plate.

To finish, garnish with the tuile, raspberry, and edible flower or mint sprig.

Peach Ice Cream

½ cup granulated sugar
6 large egg yolks
¼ teaspoon salt
½ cup heavy cream (36% M.F.)
1½ cups whole milk (3.25% M.F.)
1½ cups peeled peach cut in 1-inch pieces

In a large bowl, whisk sugar, egg yolks, and salt until pale and thick ribbons form, about 3 to 4 minutes.

Add milk and cream to a heavy-bottomed saucepan over medium heat and stirring constantly, bring liquid to a low boil.

Whisking constantly, create your custard base by gradually adding the heated cream mixture (tempering*) into the egg yolks until thoroughly incorporated. Transfer custard to the original sauce-pan and cook on medium-low, stirring frequently, until mixture thickens, but does not come to a simmer, about 4 to 5 minutes. Using a sieve, strain into a bowl and reserve.

In a blender, add peach pieces and purée until smooth. Stir purée into the reserved custard and refrigerate to chill. When fully chilled, add custard to an ice cream/sorbet maker or Pacojet* cylinder and follow manufacturer's directions to make the peach ice cream.

Yields 4¾ cups or 2 x ¾ full Pacojet beakers of ice cream

Serves 10

Vanilla Cake

¾ cup all-purpose flour
1 teaspoon baking powder
¼ teaspoon salt
¼ cup unsalted butter
½ cup granulated sugar
1 large egg
½ teaspoon vanilla extract or paste
⅜ cup whole milk (3.25% M.F.)

Preheat oven to 350°F/177°C.

In a medium bowl, sift* the flour, baking powder, and salt.

In a bowl or mixer, cream the butter and sugar over moderate speed until the mixture is light and fluffy, about 2 to 3 minutes. Add the egg and vanilla and beat until just combined.

On low speed and making three dry and two liquid additions, add the flour mixture ¼ cup at a time, alternating with the milk and the creamed butter. Combine each addition lightly but completely, being careful not to overbeat.

Coat the inside of a deep 8 x 8-inch pan with butter and dust with flour to prevent the cake from sticking. Pour the batter into the pan, level evenly with an offset spatula, and bake in the center of the oven until a toothpick inserted in the center comes out clean, about 18 to 25 minutes.
Remove cake from oven to a baking rack; run a knife tip lightly around the edge and cool. When completely cooled, use a 2-inch round cutter to cut out 6 individual rounds. Trim the rounds so they are ½-inch in height. Keep leftover cake for a snack or wrap tightly and freeze for later use.

Yields one 8 x 8-inch cake

Sous Vide Crème Brûlée

I have made hundreds of crème brûlée in my chef career and prefer to use an adaptation of the *Foolproof Crackling Crème Brûlée* recipe from Chef Steps (www.chefsteps.com). My version of the recipe, which recently won best overall dish in the International Sous Vide Association's comfort foods recipe contest, produces an unbelievably smooth and creamy textured brûlée with the perfect balance of sweetness and vanilla flavor.

To present this dessert I like to invert the brûlée and use a rectangle serving plate to accentuate its visual appeal. For a simplified version, you can leave the crème brûlée in the mason jar, brûlée, and serve.

Note: *Chef Steps* is an amazing database of recipes and techniques and is constantly being updated by very talented chefs. I highly recommend subscribing to this website.

Note: The garnishes for this dish can be made well in advance. The crème brûlée can be prepared and refrigerated at least 4 hours and up to 1 week before service

Crème Brûlée

Candied Star Fruit Slices (see Back to Basics page 216)
Dehydrated Pineapple (see Back to Basics page 221)
Sweet Crumble (see Back to Basics page 228)
Crème Anglaise (see Back to Basics page 220)
1 vanilla bean
6 tablespoons caster sugar*
11 large egg yolks
⅛ teaspoon salt
2½ cups heavy cream (36% M.F.)
6 mason jars (3-ounce size)
Vanilla Ice Cream (recipe follows)
12 mint sprigs
4 peaches or nectarines
1½ teaspoons caster sugar* (2nd amount)

Prepare the Candied Star Fruit, Dehydrated Pineapple, Sweet Crumble, and Crème Anglaise recipes in advance and reserve.

Heat sous vide bath to 176°F/80°C.

To remove seeds from the vanilla bean: run the tip of a paring knife lengthwise down the center of the bean to expose the seeds inside and split the bean into two pieces. Place the halves, skin side down, on a cutting board. Using the dull edge of a knife, run the knife down the center of each pod to remove the seeds. Add

vanilla seeds and sugar to a small bowl and combine thoroughly with your fingertips so that no clumps remain.

Note: The empty vanilla pods can be utilized to infuse various liquids or added to a jar of sugar to create vanilla-scented sugar.

In a large bowl, whisk egg yolks, vanilla sugar, and salt until well combined. Continue whisking as you slowly incorporate the heavy cream. Strain the mixture into a large clean bowl and rest 20 minutes. This ensures that all bubbles will have time to rise to the surface and dissipate. Yields 3½-cups.

Fill each mason jar with a generous ¼ cup of the liquid; reserving the remaining 2 cups liquid for the Vanilla Ice Cream recipe. Close each jar so the lid is fingertip tight. When the sous vide bath is at proper temperature, use tongs to submerge each jar into the bath in an upright position. Do not be alarmed if bubbles rise to the surface of the water bath as this is air escaping from the jars. Sous vide for 1 hour.

Prepare Vanilla Ice Cream (recipe follows).

Using tongs, remove mason jars from the water bath and place on countertop. After 15 minutes, remove the lids to ensure that condensation does not develop and then allow the jars to cool to the touch. When the jars have completely cooled, about 35 to 45 minutes, replace and tighten the lids. Reserve jars in refrigerator

for at least 4 hours and up to 1 week before service.

Rinse mint sprigs, pat dry, and reserve. Slice peaches or nectarines into 24 wedges and 12 cubes for plating; refrigerate ingredients.

Service

Remove Vanilla Ice Cream from freezer to soften for service. If using a Pacojet*, pacotize the ice cream reserved in the beaker.

Fill a tall glass with hot water and insert a thin paring knife to warm. Remove the crème brûlée jars from refrigerator and run the tip of the knife around the edge of each brûlée 3 to 4 times; cleaning the knife with a paper towel after each rotation. Invert each brûlée onto small individual plates and if necessary, tidy and re-mold each with a damp finger. Dust the top of each brûlée with ¼ teaspoon caster sugar* (2nd amount). Using a kitchen torch, torch each brûlée until the sugar has caramelized and is golden brown.

Remove all reserved ingredients from refrigerator for plating.

To Plate

Using a pastry brush, "paint" the Crème Anglaise onto the base of the plate. Scatter three mounds of the crumble onto the plate and lightly flatten. Carefully transfer the crème brûlée to the plate and garnish with the peach or nectarine. Mold the ice cream into a quenelle* shape and lay on one of the flattened crumble mounds. This will absorb the melted ice cream and keep the quenelle* static on the plate.

To finish, garnish with the star fruit, pineapple, and mint sprigs.

Serves 6

Vanilla Ice Cream

2 cups reserved cream liquid from the Crème Brûlée

Fill an ice cream/sorbet maker or Pacojet* cylinder and follow manufacturer's directions to make the vanilla ice cream.

Desserts   **205**

Tiered Chocolate Mousse

This dessert is a combination of two recipes featured in the book. Using your creative imagination, it is possible to mix and match components of each recipe to create a new signature dessert of your own. Feel free to substitute the acetate strip with a mold of your choice, or for a simplified serving version, divide the prepared mousse between eight individual serving dishes, chill and serve.

To garnish this dish, I use stencils I have collected over the years. My favorite are Martha Stewart's adhesive stencils that can be found online or at various craft stores. To add another element to the dish, I also like to cover the dessert with a glass cloche dome and smoke with cherrywood chips.

Note: The components for this dish can be made well in advance. The chocolate mousse mold will need to be prepared at least 24 hours and up to 1 month in advance.

Note: For a simplified plating option, divide the mousse between six individual serving dishes, cover, and chill until set, at least 2 hours. This serving option will omit the need to freeze the mousse as there will be no need to remove them from the acetate mold. Bear in mind that this option will not give you the same exquisite dessert presentation.

¾ cup Healthy Dried Fruit Truffle base (see recipe on page 195)
4 ounces (113.5 grams) milk, bittersweet or dark chocolate, ½-inch pieces or callets* (preferably couverture chocolate*)
7 tablespoons (3½ ounces) unsalted butter
2 large eggs, separated
1 tablespoon granulated sugar
¾ cup heavy cream (36% M.F.)
Pinch of salt
6 teaspoons chocolate torte base (see recipe on page 182) or 6 store-bought chocolate truffles, 1-inch diameter with a flat bottom
Almond Tuile (recipe follows)
Chocolate Sauce (see Back to Basics page 218)
Raspberry Coulis (see Back to Basics page 227)
6 raspberries
6 small mint leaves
2 tablespoons Dutch cocoa powder

Prepare the Healthy Dried Fruit Truffle base and reserve in refrigerator.

In a small heavy-bottomed saucepan, heat 1-inch of water to simmer. Place the chocolate and butter in a medium heatproof bowl and set over the simmering water; this is the double boiler* method (see Crème Anglaise recipe in Back to Basics for more description). Stir the chocolate until completely melted, remove from the double boiler* and cool until tepid.

Using an electric mixer, whisk egg whites on medium-high speed till soft peaks form, about 1 to 2 minutes. Gradually beat in caster sugar, 1 teaspoon at a time, until sugar is dissolved and stiff, glossy peaks form, about 2 to 3 minutes; be careful not to overbeat. Transfer whites to a clean bowl and reserve.
Thoroughly clean the mixer bowl and whisk. Add cream to mixer bowl and beat until soft peaks form.

In another bowl large enough to hold all ingredients, thoroughly combine the egg yolks and salt. Using a rubber spatula, stir the cooled chocolate mixture into the egg yolks; gently fold in the whipped egg whites and the whipping cream, combining until no streaks remain.

Remove the Healthy Dried Fruit Truffle base from refrigerator and shape into a disk. If the mixture is difficult to shape, allow it to rest and warm on the counter for a few minutes. Place the disk between two pieces of plastic wrap and using a rolling pin, roll the disk until it has an even flat surface and is ¼-inch thick. Using a 2-inch ring mold, cut 6 rounds from the disk and refrigerate until firm, about 12 minutes. Use the excess dried fruit mixture as a healthy snack, or freeze and reserve for later use.

Prepare 6 individual 2 x 9-inch strips of acetate. Wrap 1 strip around the edge of each disk to create a 2-inch diameter casing. Hold the strip in place and completely wrap the circumference with tape to secure the acetate ring.

Fill each mold with the chocolate mousse. Using an offset spatula, press firmly down on the mousse to eliminate air pockets. Level the mousse, cover with plastic wrap, and freeze overnight or until completely solid.

Note: The individual chocolate mousse will need to defrost in the refrigerator 3 to 4 hours prior to service.

Prepare the chocolate truffles: if using the chocolate torte base, roll 6 chocolate truffles 1 inch in diameter with a flat base for a static placement. If using store-bought truffles, ensure that they have a flat bottom. Cover and reserve truffles on the counter for service.

Prepare the Almond Tuile, Chocolate Sauce, and Raspberry Coulis.

Rinse, pat dry, and reserve raspberries and mint leaves in the refrigerator.

Service

Remove mousse from the freezer and remove their acetate strips. Place mousse on small individual plates and defrost 3 to 4 hours in refrigerator.

Cut ⅓ off the top of each raspberry so you have a visible hole throughout each piece of fruit. Tuck one mint leaf into each hole so that half of the mint leaf is exposed and standing tall.

Add Dutch cocoa to a small bowl; toss each truffle in the cocoa to coat.

Optional: prepare a hand smoker with cherrywood chips and have ready for plating.

To Plate

I use a stencil to garnish the rim of this plate. Press your stencil of choice firmly on the plate and with a small paintbrush, "paint" the chocolate sauce onto the stencil. Dust with cocoa, tap to remove excess powder and remove the stencil.
I like to use a dry paintbrush to finish and perfect the shape. Finish garnishing the rim of the plate with a squeeze bottle filled with the Chocolate Sauce.

Spoon the Raspberry Coulis onto the center of each serving dish and spread into a 2¼-inch round base.

Place a mousse in the center of each plate, top with the Almond Tuile, truffle, raspberry, and mint leaf.

Optional: cover each dessert with a dome and gently fill domes with the cherrywood smoke. Serve immediately.

Serves 6

Almond Tuile

If baking tuiles in advance, store them in a lidded airtight container at room temperature. This recipe makes a large batch. Portion and freeze the excess dough to use with a variety of desserts.

⅔ cup confectioner's sugar
2 tablespoons all-purpose flour
4 teaspoons water
4½ teaspoons honey
2 tablespoons + 2 teaspoons unsalted butter
150 grams (5.3 ounces) sliced almonds, chopped

Preheat oven to 325°F/163°C.

Sift* the confectioner's sugar and flour into a medium bowl.

Combine water, honey, and butter in a small saucepan over medium-low heat and whisk until the butter has melted and the honey has completely dissolved.

Stir the honey mixture into the powdered sugar until thoroughly combined; fold in the chopped almonds. Refrigerate the batter for 30 to 60 minutes. This will allow it to firm up before use.

Line a baking sheet with a Silpat* or parchment paper. Drop batter from a tablespoon about 4 inches apart on the baking sheet. Use the back of the spoon to lightly flatten the tuiles into 2-inch rounds.

Bake in preheated oven until lightly browned around the edges, about 12 to 15 minutes. Immediately remove baking sheet from oven and allow tuiles to cool on the baking sheet. When cooled, remove tuiles with an offset spatula and reserve in an airtight container.

View from Cane Garden Bay, Tortola

BACK TO BASICS

Back to Basics is a compilation of culinary components that I always have readily available in my kitchen or freezer each day. Having ingredients such as these on hand for everyday use can elevate even the simplest dish into a gourmet experience. Take the time to prepare these recipes in advance and eliminate the need to prepare the day of service, saving you a great deal of time and energy.

Balsamic Glaze

This glaze is a perfect balance between the acidic taste of vinegar and the sweetness of brown sugar. It has a beautiful charcoal color and a perfect consistency for garnishing many dishes. This is a staple in my pantry that I keep readily available in a squeeze bottle to decorate plates for service.

2 cups balsamic vinegar
2 tablespoons brown sugar

In a medium heavy-bottomed saucepan, bring vinegar to a low simmer and reduce liquid to ½ cup, about 20 to 30 minutes. Whisk in brown sugar, stirring constantly, until sugar is dissolved. Turn burner to low, simmer, and continue to reduce until desired consistency is reached, about 15 to 20 minutes.

Note: Once the mixture cools it will thicken, as well.

Remove from heat, cool and transfer to a squeeze bottle. If the glaze is too thick, simply reheat and add more vinegar for the desired consistency. It will keep refrigerated for up to two weeks.

Yields ½ cup

Balsamic Vinegar Pearls

2 cups olive oil
⅔ cup balsamic vinegar
2 grams agar agar*
Syringe or eyedropper

Pour olive oil into a tall glass and place in freezer so that it becomes very cold but not frozen, about 30 minutes. The oil must be extremely cold for the balsamic pearls to become small, well-formed pearls by the time they reach the bottom of the glass.

Once the oil is chilled, combine vinegar and agar agar* in a small saucepan. Stirring constantly, bring mixture to a boil and then immediately remove from heat. Cool slightly, about 5 minutes.

Remove oil from the freezer. Fill a syringe or eyedropper with vinegar mixture and slowly drip the mixture into the oil. Repeat the process with remaining vinegar mixture.

Gently strain pearls from the olive oil and lightly rinse with water. Refrigerate in a container.

If you would like to make the Balsamic Vinegar Pearls in advance, store the pearls in the refrigerator in the olive oil.

Basil Oil

Herb-infused oils give richness, flavor, and body to any dish. There are numerous variations and the flavor produced is well worth the effort. Use herb oils to drizzle over your favorite dishes, produce robust vinaigrettes, or just place on the table for everyday use. Herb oils are best if they are made 24 hours in advance to service, and can be frozen for later use.

3 cups packed basil leaves
¾ cup vegetable oil*, portioned

Prepare ice bath in advance by combining ice and water in a small bowl.

Bring a small saucepan of salted water to a boil (1½ tablespoons salt per quart of water). Add basil and blanch 15 seconds. Drain and immediately plunge leaves into ice water bath to stop the cooking process and to retain the vibrant green color. Strain leaves and squeeze as much of the water out as possible. If water remains, wrap the leaves in a paper towel, squeeze and wring to remove excess water.

Place half the leaves in a blender with enough oil just to cover. Turn the blender on medium and blend for one minute. Place the remaining leaves in the blender, turn the speed to high and continue to blend for 30 seconds. Remove the top of the blender and slowly add the remaining oil in a steady stream. Blend for 4 to 5 minutes.

Add oil and leaves to a lidded airtight container and refrigerate for 2–24 hours to allow the color and flavor to intensify. **Note:** The flavor will intensify the longer the oil is allowed to infuse.

To finish: strain basil oil through a fine mesh strainer lined with cheesecloth*. Allow oil to filter without pressure, about an hour. Discard the cheesecloth*, being careful not to wring the cloth or allow any basil residue to enter, discolor, or cloud the final product. Pour oil into a squeeze bottle; refrigerate up to two days.

Note: Refrigerated Basil Oil can be made up to a week in advance by reserving the unstrained puréed mixture in an airtight container and straining the day of service, or freeze the unstrained puree for later use.

Yields 1 cup

Béchamel

Béchamel is one of the five French "mother sauces." This white sauce arose during the reign of Louis XIV and has been the base for many sauces since that time. Béchamel is praised for its consistency and satiny finish.

2¾ cups whole milk (3.25 % M.F.)
½ small onion, peeled, halved
4 whole cloves
1 bay leaf
2 tablespoons unsalted butter
3½ tablespoons all-purpose flour
½ teaspoon salt
⅛ teaspoon white pepper

In a small heavy-bottomed saucepan, heat the milk, halved onion (studded with cloves) and bay leaf to a simmer. Cover, remove from heat, and steep for 20 minutes.

In a medium saucepan, melt the butter over low heat; stirring constantly, add the flour and cook 2 minutes. This will make a roux*. Using a strainer fitted over the saucepan, add the steeped milk in a steady stream, whisking constantly to avoid lumps. Continue to cook on low heat at a low simmer until the desired consistency is achieved, about 6 to 8 minutes. Adjust seasoning with salt and pepper.

Yields 2 cups

Beurre Monté

This form of butter is a perfect way to poach fish, meat, or vegetables. Normally, butter cannot be heated above 160°F/71°C without separating, but using this method will allow you to raise the heating point to 190°F/88°C without separation of solids.

Beurre Monté is also used as a base or to finish a variety of sauces. It creates a smooth taste and gives any sauce a full body shine. Leftover Beurre Monté can be turned into clarified butter or chilled in the refrigerator and used the same way you would whole butter. Beurre Monté is a multipurpose tool for every kitchen and very easy to prepare.

2 tablespoons water
2 tablespoons to 1 pound unsalted butter, cubed and chilled

Just 2 tablespoons of water, regardless of the butter quantity, is all you need to make Beurre Monté. In a saucepan, heat the water to a simmer and immediately whisk in chilled butter pieces one at a time. Once finished, keep the Beurre Monté at room temperature to ensure its consistency. Excess Beurre Monté can also be refrigerated for later use.

Candied Fruit Slices

I use only firm fruit for this recipe to ensure that it stays structurally intact during the poaching and dehydrating process.

1 whole semi-ripe fruit (apple, pear, star fruit, citrus, etc.)
1 cup sugar
2 cups water

Preheat oven to 225°F/107°C.

With a mandolin, thinly slice unpeeled fruit using the 1.5 mm setting.

In a small heavy-bottomed saucepan, combine sugar and water; stir to dissolve and bring liquid to a low simmer. Add the sliced fruit to the simmering liquid, one piece at a time, to ensure the slices do not stick together; cook for 8 to 10 minutes, while not allowing the liquid to boil. Remove saucepan from heat; leave fruit slices in the liquid and cool.

When cool, using a slotted spoon, remove slices one at a time, shaking off the excess poaching liquid. Individually fan the fruit slices onto a Silpat*- or parchment paper-lined baking sheet, making sure they do not overlap. Place baking sheet in oven; dehydrate the fruit, flipping after the first hour and then every 30 minutes for 2½ to 3 hours, until they are crisp and translucent. Remove from oven, cool slices and store in an airtight container with tight-fitting lid for up to 1 month.

Note: The poaching liquid may be used as simple syrup*; strain the liquid and reserve in the refrigerator

Chocolate Crumble

This recipe is the chocolate version of the Sweet Crumble. It is a delicious garnish for ice cream, sorbet, and other desserts.

½ cup unsalted butter, chilled, cut into ½-inch cubes
1 cup all-purpose flour
¼ cup Dutch cocoa powder
½ cup granulated sugar
Pinch salt

Preheat oven to 375°F/190°C.

In a medium bowl, combine all ingredients and process, using your fingers or a pastry cutter, until the mixture resembles coarse sand.

Spread the crumble evenly onto a Silpat*- or parchment paper-lined baking sheet. Bake the crumble, stirring the mixture and rotating the baking sheet after 10 minutes. Continue baking until mixture is crunchy, about 8 to 10 minutes longer. Remove from oven, cool and store in an airtight container or Ziplock bag for up to 1 month.

Chocolate Garnish (tempering* chocolate)

It is not difficult to temper chocolate; all you need is a thermometer and either a chocolate melter or glass bowl. **Note:** Try to use high-quality couverture chocolate* for melting as it contains a higher percentage of cocoa butter than regular baking or eating chocolate.

To make the garnishes: measure any amount of one variety of the following: dark, milk, or white callets*, or ½-inch pieces of chocolate. Portion the chocolate: 95% for the initial melting and 5% to be used for tempering.

The first step is to melt the chocolate using a chocolate melter, double boiler*, direct heat, or the microwave to a temperature of 113°F/45°C.

Once the chocolate has risen to the correct temperature, lower the heat or remove from heat until the chocolate lowers to 88°F/31°C for dark chocolate and 84°F/29°C for milk chocolate and white chocolate. At this point, immediately add the reserved 5% chocolate and stir until smooth. **Note:** If the 5% chocolate melts too quickly, it means the temperature of the melted chocolate is still too high. Remedy this by stirring an additional small handful of chocolate into the mixture. Once all of the chocolate is completely melted and smooth, you will have a working product.

To check whether the chocolate has tempered properly simply drizzle a spoonful of the chocolate onto a Silpat* or parchment paper and set aside at room temperature. If after 2 to 3 minutes, the chocolate hardens, loses its sheen, and breaks with a nice snap, then the chocolate is ready. At this stage, working quickly, create your choice of chocolate garnishes to garnish any dessert.

Chocolate Sauce

This dessert sauce has a perfect consistency for garnishing many dishes and is a staple in my pantry. I keep it readily available in a squeeze bottle to decorate plates for service.

1 cup water
½ cup granulated sugar
½ cup corn syrup, agave nectar, or glucose syrup
¾ cup Dutch cocoa powder
56.7 grams (2 ounces) bittersweet chocolate, pieces, or callets*
(preferably coverture chocolate*)

In a small heavy-bottomed saucepan, whisk together water, sugar, syrup, and cocoa powder. Heat the mixture, whisking frequently, until it comes to a boil. Remove from heat, stir in the chopped chocolate until thoroughly combined and cool. When cooled, transfer sauce to a squeeze bottle and refrigerate for up to 2 weeks.

Cilantro Oil

3 cups packed cilantro leaves
¾ cup vegetable oil* (portioned)

Prepare ice bath in advance by combining ice and water in a small bowl.

Bring a small saucepan of salted water to a boil (1½ tablespoons salt per quart of water). Add cilantro leaves and blanch for 15 seconds. Drain and immediately plunge leaves into ice bath to stop the cooking process and retain the vibrant green color. Strain leaves and squeeze as much of the water out as possible. If water remains, wrap the leaves in a paper towel, squeeze and wring to remove excess.

Place half the leaves in a blender with enough oil just to cover. Turn the blender on medium and blend for one minute. Place the remaining leaves in the blender, turn the speed to high and continue to blend, 30 seconds. Remove the top of the blender and slowly add the remaining oil in a steady stream. Blend for 4 to 5 minutes.

Add oil and leaves to a lidded airtight container and refrigerate 24 hours to allow the color and flavor to intensify.

To finish, strain cilantro oil through a fine mesh strainer lined with cheesecloth*. Allow oil to filter without pressure, about an hour. Discard the cheesecloth*, being careful not to wring cloth or allow any cilantro residue to enter, discolor, or cloud the final product. Pour oil into a squeeze bottle; refrigerate up to two days.

Note: Refrigerated Cilantro Oil can be made up to a week in advance by reserving the unstrained puréed mixture in an airtight container and straining the day of service, or freeze the unstrained purée for later use.

Yields 1 cup

Clarified Butter (Ghee)

Butter consists of at least 80% milk fat, 16 to 18% water, and 1 to 2% milk solids. When you heat butter above 160°F/71°C, the components separate.

454g (1 pound) unsalted butter

In a heavy-bottomed saucepan, melt butter over low heat; do not stir and do not allow to simmer or boil. When the butter has melted, skim* and discard the foamy milk solids that have risen to the surface. There will be three layers: the foaming milk solids, the clear butterfat, and the milky liquid at the bottom. Once you have discarded all of the foam, carefully pour the clear butterfat into a container, leaving the milky liquid behind.

The final product is a beautiful clear, rich, golden butterfat. Because it no longer contains any solid state, this product can be used at a higher heat point without burning. During the process, you will loss about ¼ of the original butter product. Store refrigerated, in a lidded airtight container for up to one month.

Yields 1½ cups

Court Bouillon

1½ tablespoons crab boil mix *, Penzeys spices or other commercial brand
1 teaspoon whole black peppercorns
2 parsley stems
4 thyme stems
7 cups water
2 cups dry white wine, *Hahn Pinot Gris*
1 large carrot, cut in 1-inch pieces
1 celery rib, cut in 1-inch pieces
¼ large onion, cut in 1-inch dice
1 lemon, halved and juiced

Take a 4 x 4-inch piece of cheesecloth* and lay it flat on the counter to make the bouqet garni*. Place the crab boil mix*, whole peppercorns, and fresh herbs in the center of the cheesecloth and tie the four corners together with butcher's twine*.

Fill a large stockpot with the bouquet garni*, water, wine, vegetables, lemon, and lemon juice. Bring the court bouillon to a boil, reduce heat and simmer for 10 minutes. Remove stockpot from heat, cover and allow the liquid to cool and infuse the flavors. The court bouillon can be made in advance and refrigerated for later use.

Crème Anglaise

1 vanilla bean
2 tablespoons caster sugar*
1 cup heavy cream (36% M.F.)
½ cup whole milk (3.25% M.F.)
½ cup egg yolks, from about 6 large eggs
Pinch salt

For this recipe it is ideal to use a double boiler*. To make your own double boiler* at home you will need a deep saucepan and a glass or metal bowl that will rest suspended on the rim of the pan leaving at least a 3-inch gap from the bottom. To use the double boiler*, you will need 1- to 2-inches of water in the bottom of the saucepan. Set the bowl over the water, heat to a low simmer, being careful not to boil. The steam will rise, heating the bottom of the bowl to create a slow cooking effect.

Prepare an ice bath in advance by combining ice and water in a bowl that is slightly larger that the bowl you will use for the double boiler*. You will use the ice bath at the end of the recipe to flash chill the Crème Anglaise.

Run the tip of a pairing knife lengthwise down the center of the vanilla bean to expose the seeds, split the bean into two halves and place skin side down on a cutting board. Using the dull edge of a knife, run the knife down the center of each pod to remove the seeds.

Note: The empty vanilla pods can be utilized to infuse various liquids or added to a jar of sugar to create vanilla-scented sugar.

In a small bowl, using your fingertips, thoroughly combine the vanilla seeds and sugar so that no clumps remain.

In the bowl for the double boiler*, thoroughly whisk together the vanilla sugar, cream, milk, egg yolk, and salt. Place the bowl on top of the saucepan; insert a thermometer into the crème mixture so that you can continuously read the temperature and bring pan to a low simmer. While whisking, heat the mixture to 176°F/80°C. The desired viscosity should be thick enough to coat the back of a spoon. When temperature is reached, remove bowl from saucepan and submerge only the base of the bowl into the prepared ice bath. Stirring constantly, cool the anglaise to room temperature. When cooled, strain the mixture through a sieve and reserve for service.

This recipe will make more than what is required for one dish. I like to portion the sauce and freeze for later use. To reuse, thaw the sauce and then slowly bring it to the desired temperature on the stovetop or serve at room temperature. Never allow Crème Anglaise to come to a boil or the sauce will split.

Dehydrated Pineapple

½ whole pineapple

Preheat the oven to 225°F/107°C.

Line three 11.5 x 15.5-inch baking sheets with Silpats* or parchment paper. Using a serrated knife, remove the crown, skin, and eyes of the pineapple. Using a mandolin* or knife, thinly slice the fruit into 1.5 mm slices. Individually fan the slices onto baking sheets so they do not overlap.

Place baking sheets in oven; dehydrate the fruit, flipping after the first hour and then every 30 minutes for 1½ to 2 hours until completely dried. Remove from oven, cool slices and store in a lidded airtight container for up to one month.

Gelatin

• 1 envelope of granulated gelatin is ¼ ounce or 2¼ teaspoons.

• 1 envelope firmly sets 2 cups of liquid and is ideal to unmold a dessert.

• 1 envelope softly sets 3 cups of liquid.

• Always dissolve granulated gelatin in cold water.

• Never heat a set gelatin dessert as it will melt.

• Desserts made with gelatin will need at least 8 to 24 hours to fully set.

• Certain raw tropical fruits have an enzyme that will keep gelatin from setting, to resolve this issue, heat the fruit to kill the enzyme.

Grilled Vegetables

⅓ cup + ¼ cup extra virgin olive oil
1¼ teaspoons smoked Spanish paprika
1 teaspoon brown sugar
1 teaspoon Italian herbs
¼ teaspoon garlic powder
¾ teaspoon salt
¼ teaspoon black pepper
2 bell peppers, trimmed, seeded, cut into 6 lengthwise strips
2 zucchinis, trimmed, cut lengthwise ¼-inch slices
1 small Italian eggplant, trimmed, cut in ¼-inch slices
8 cremini mushrooms, halved
1 small onion, trimmed, cut in ½-inch rounds

Preheat grill to medium-high heat 375°F/190°C to 400°F/204°C. Make sure grill is clean and piping hot.

In a small bowl, whisk together olive oil, smoked Spanish paprika, brown sugar, Italian herbs, garlic powder, salt and pepper.

In a large bowl, combine all the prepared vegetables and the oil mixture; toss and coat thoroughly.

Grill the vegetables, flipping every 4 to 5 minutes until cooked through, about 15 to 30 minutes depending on the temperature of your grill. When cooked, remove from heat.

Note: There are many ways to serve these delicious grilled vegetables; cube and stir in chopped tomatoes for a ratatouille, chill for an antipasto dish, or roll into the delicious Italian Sushi (page 58). The vegetables may also be frozen for later use.

Hahn GSM Onion Chutney

1 large sweet onion (Vidalia, Walla Walla, etc.)
1 tablespoon extra virgin olive oil
3 tablespoons brown sugar
1 cup full-bodied red wine, *Hahn GSM wine*
3 tablespoons Balsamic Glaze (see page 213)
½ teaspoon dried Italian herbs
½ teaspoon dried thyme
¼ teaspoon ground black pepper
1 cup beef consommé*

Remove the stem of the onion, peel and halve lengthwise. Cut into ¼-inch slices; separate each slice to yield about 3 to 3½ cups onion.

In a 12-inch sauté pan, heat olive oil over medium heat. Add onion to pan, reduce heat to medium low; cover and cook, stirring every few minutes until transparent, about 10 minutes. Remove cover, add the sugar and cook, stirring every 5 minutes, until onions are caramelized, about 35 minutes.

Add the wine, Balsamic Glaze, dried herbs, pepper, and consommé*; bring to a low simmer and cook, stirring occasionally, until thickened and desired consistency is achieved, about 50 to 60 minutes. **Note:** Refrigerate chutney in a lidded airtight container for up to one week, or portion and freeze for up to 4 months.

Yields 1 cup

Honey Dijonnaise

1 tablespoon apple cider vinegar
1½ tablespoons liquid honey
⅜ cup Mayonnaise (see page 224)
2 teaspoons Dijon mustard
2 teaspoons grainy mustard
⅛ teaspoon Worcestershire sauce*
¼ cup vegetable oil*
1 teaspoon finely chopped fresh parsley or other fresh herbs
Salt

In a medium bowl, whisk together the cider vinegar and honey until thoroughly combined.

Whisk the Mayonnaise and mustards into the vinegar mixture until well blended. With a whisk, slowly beat in the vegetable oil until the mixture is emulsified and thick.

Stir in parsley and adjust seasoning with salt to taste. Store in a plastic squeeze bottle, refrigerated, for up to 2 weeks. Bring to room temperature to serve.

Yields ¾ cup

Mayonnaise

1 large egg yolk
½ to 1 teaspoon Dijon mustard
½ teaspoon salt
¼ cup vegetable oil*
1 teaspoon white wine vinegar
1 teaspoon water (optional)
2 teaspoons lemon juice
½ cup vegetable oil* (2nd amount)

In a medium bowl, whisk the yolk, preferred amount of mustard, and salt until thoroughly combined. Whisking constantly, add ¼ cup of the vegetable oil, drop by drop, until emulsified and thickened. Whisk in the vinegar and lemon juice.

Whisking constantly, add the remaining vegetable oil in a slow, steady stream. If at any point the mayonnaise is not emulsifying, stop the flow of oil and mix vigorously to re-emulsify. Resume adding the oil until the mixture is thoroughly combined and emulsified. Adjust seasoning again if necessary. Store refrigerated in a lidded airtight container for up to 5 days.

Yields ⅞ cup

Molecular Caviars

Molecular spherification were originally created for the pharmaceutical industry during the 1950s. This jellifying technique was then
mastered and refined by *Chef Ferran Adria* of the legendary El Bulli Restaurant. At the turn of the 20th century, *Chef Adria's* refined cuisine and evolutionary molecular gastronomy changed modern cuisine to what we know today.

The main active gelling ingredient that creates the thin membrane or "caviar shape" around your liquid of choice is an extraction of brown algae called sodium alginate*. When used with a calcium lactate* or calcium chloride* bath, a simple gelling reaction takes place, creating wonderful spheres that essentially "pop" in your mouth. There are two different techniques for the spherification process: Basic Spherification and Reverse Spherification. Both follow the same methods, but it may be more ideal to use one over the other based on the level of acidity, alcohol, or calcium in the flavor liquid of choice.

Note: When the liquid of choice is too acidic (or has a low PH level), sodium citrate* is added to the liquid to increase the PH level to above 3.6. This is only necessary when using acidic ingredients that retain a low PH level.

For Direct (Basic) Spherification, a 0.5 to 1.0% sodium alginate* base is used with a 0.5% to 1% calcium setting bath.

Note: I purchase all molecular products online from Modernist Pantry.

Citrus Caviar (Direct or Basic Spherification)

200 grams yuzu, lemon, or grapefruit juice
1 gram sodium alginate*
1 teaspoon sodium citrate*
2½ cups (600 grams) cold distilled water
3 grams calcium chloride*
4 cups room temperature distilled water (2nd amount)

In a medium bowl, sprinkle the sodium alginate* and sodium citrate* over the citrus juice and blend with a hand blender to thoroughly incorporate, about 8 to 10 minutes. Strain, cover and refrigerate the mixture for at least 2 hours to allow the bubbles to rise to the surface and to rehydrate the sodium alginate*.

For the calcium chloride* bath: sprinkle the calcium chloride* over 2½ cups cold distilled water and stir or blend with hand blender until completely dissolved. Cover and refrigerate for at least 15 minutes prior to use.

Place 4 cups distilled water (2nd amount) in a third separate bowl; this will be used to rinse the caviar.

Set on the counter and in front of you, the sodium alginate* mixture, calcium bath, and bowl with 2nd amount of distilled water.

Just before use, gently stir the citrus mixture. Fill a syringe or eyedropper with the citrus mixture to the halfway point. Drop this solution into the calcium bath, one small drop at a time, from a height of between ¼ to 1 inch above the water. The "caviar" will sink to the bottom of the bath; stir gently and leave caviar for 1 minute to produce a thin membrane. Using a perforated spoon, remove caviar from the bath and rinse for 1 to 3 minutes. Remove caviar using the slotted spoon and serve immediately. **Note:** The caviar will solidify completely after fifteen minutes. It will still be possible to use, but will not have the same "pop" when eaten.

Oven-Dried Cherry Tomatoes

Once dehydrated, the tomato halves will have around a 25% size reduction. They will take on a beautiful deep red hue and develop an intense burst of tomato flavor. They are a wonderful addition to any dish, visually appealing and packed with flavor. To make a large amount, dehydrate tomatoes and when cool, pack in a jar or airtight container, add fresh herbs, salt and pepper, and completely cover with extra virgin olive oil. When tomatoes are covered in oil that may be stored in refrigerator for up to a month.

12 cherry tomatoes
1 teaspoon extra virgin olive oil
Salt and pepper

Preheat oven to 200°F/93°C.

Halve cherry tomatoes and place, cut side up, on a Silpat*- or parchment-lined baking sheet. Dehydrate the tomatoes in the oven until they are semi-dehydrated, about 3 hours. Drizzle tomatoes with olive oil, season with salt and pepper, and reserve for service.

Pesto Alla Genovese

2 cups packed basil leaves
2 small garlic cloves, peeled
½ teaspoon salt
½ cup toasted pine nuts
¼ teaspoon freshly ground black pepper
¼ cup grated pecorino cheese, preferably Sardinian
¼ cup grated Parmigiano-Reggiano cheese
½ cup extra virgin olive oil

Prepare ice bath in advance by combining ice and water in a small bowl.

Bring a saucepan of salted water to a boil (1½ tablespoons salt per quart of water).
Add basil and blanch 15 seconds. Drain and immediately plunge leaves into ice bath to stop the cooking process and retain the vibrant green color. Strain leaves and squeeze as much of the water out as possible.

Using a food processor, process the garlic and salt into a smooth paste. While pulsing, gradually add the basil leaves, pine nuts, black pepper, and both cheeses. With the blender running, add the olive oil in a slow steady stream, processing until completely incorporated. Adjust viscosity with olive oil and seasoning with salt.

Note: Refrigerate pesto in a lidded airtight container for up to one week, or portion and freeze for up to 4 months.

Pork Tenderloin Brine

Yields 7 cups of liquid, enough brine for 2 tenderloins
Note: This brine can also be used to add additional flavor and seasoning to a variety of proteins.

1 teaspoon whole black peppercorns
1 tablespoon crab boil mix *, Penzeys or other commercial brand
8 fresh parsley stems
4 fresh thyme stems or ½ teaspoon dried thyme
4 cups of water
½ cup salt
½ cup brown sugar
4 cups ice

Take an 8 x 8-inch piece of cheesecloth* and lay it flat on the counter. Place the peppercorns, crab boil mix*, and fresh herbs in the center of the cheesecloth and tie the four corners together to make a bouquet garni*.

Heat 4 cups of water, salt, sugar, and bouquet garni* in a medium heavy-bottomed saucepan. Bring to a boil, reduce to a simmer and stir occasionally until the salt and sugar have dissolved, about 3 to 4 minutes.

Remove the pot from heat and cool liquid to room temperature. Add the 4 cups of ice and stir until the temperature of the liquid has dropped below 41°F/5°C. At this time, add your pork to the brining mixture for up to 8 hours. **Note:** If the temperature of the brine rises above 41°F/5°C, refrigerate immediately.

When brine is complete, remove the tenderloins from the liquid and pat dry. At this time, you can marinate, cook, or freeze the tenderloins for later use.

Raspberry Coulis

Coulis consist of a fruit purée that has been thinned with simple syrup*. They are very diverse and can be made from almost any variety of fruit. To ensure maximum flavor and color, use fresh fruit and purée to a smooth consistency in a blender. It is also possible to infuse a simple syrup* with your flavor of choice; simply add the flavor prior to bringing the simple syrup* to a boil, and strain once cool.

Note: The simple syrup will make more than what is required for this recipe store in the fridge for up to one week or freeze for future use.

SIMPLE SYRUP
½ cup water
½ cup granulated white sugar

Combine the ingredients in a heavy-bottomed saucepan. Bring to a boil, stirring frequently, until the sugar is completely dissolved. Cool and reserve in refrigerator.

RASPBERRY COULIS
6 ounces (170 grams) raspberries
2 tablespoons Simple Syrup* (recipe above)

Using a blender, purée the raspberries and simple syrup* until smooth. Strain purée through a fine-mesh sieve and transfer to a squeeze bottle for serving. Store in the refrigerator for up to 3 days, or portion and freeze for future use.

Yields ¾ cup

Roux

Roux* is the classic French thickening agent for soups and sauces. The general rule to produce a roux* is by weight, using equal parts all-purpose flour and fat. Butter is the most commonly used fat, but it is possible to substitute with oil, bacon grease, or other rendered lards. In this recipe, we are producing a white roux*, but there are three varieties of roux* utilized in different methods of cuisine: white, blond, and brown roux*. The different colors result from how long the roux* has been cooked over low heat.

2 tablespoons unsalted butter
3½ tablespoons all-purpose flour

In a small heavy-bottomed saucepan, heat butter over medium heat until melted and just starting to bubble, lower heat if necessary. Immediately whisk in the flour, 1 teaspoon at a time, until roux is thoroughly incorporated and forms a thick paste. Whisk constantly and continue to cook for 5 minutes. Remove from heat and cool. If you are not using the roux* immediately, it can be stored in refrigerator up to 2 weeks or freezer for months.

Soy Glaze

½ cup soy sauce
1 teaspoon cornstarch

Combine all ingredients in a small heavy-bottomed saucepan; whisk to thoroughly combine and bring to a simmer. Remove from heat and cool. Strain the liquid and transfer to squeeze bottle for service. The glaze can be made up to 2 days in advance, store refrigerated.

Yields ⅓ cup

Sweet Crumble

This basic sweet crumble is very versatile. The crumble can be used to top any stewed fruit such as apple, blackberry, rhubarb, or peach: simply add the topping and bake.

Note: For an additional flavor profile, add ½ teaspoon of a ground spice such as cinnamon, star anise*, clove, or five spice.

For this recipe, I bake in advance and allow it to cool. It is then used to garnish a plethora of desserts giving them additional flavor and crunch.

½ cup cold unsalted butter, ½-inch cubes
1¼ cups all-purpose flour
½ cup granulated sugar
Pinch salt

Preheat oven to 375°F/190°C.

In a medium bowl, combine all ingredients and process, using your fingers or a pastry cutter, until the mixture resembles coarse sand.

Spread the crumble evenly, onto a Silpat*- or parchment paper-lined baking sheet. Bake the crumble, stirring the mixture and rotating the baking sheet after 10 minutes. Continue baking until mixture is crunchy, about 8 to 10 minutes longer. Remove from oven, cool and store in an airtight container or Ziplock bag for up to 1 month.

Vanilla and Chocolate Tuile

This tuile recipe will make a rather large batch. Prepare, portion, and freeze for various desserts. Use this recipe as a base, create your desired shape and dust* with anything from cocoa powder, coconut, crushed brittle, or nuts. Plastic lids or leftover Silpat* sheets make perfect stencils for your tuiles. Simply draw your design and cut. Shape the tuiles by draping the hot cookies over a rolling pin, glass, or empty egg carton.

1 vanilla bean
1¾ cups confectioner's sugar, sifted*
6 tablespoons (3 ounces) unsalted butter at room temperature
Egg whites from 3½ large eggs
¾ cup + 3 tablespoons all-purpose flour (Optional: To create chocolate tuiles, substitute 4 tablespoons of flour for 5 tablespoons Dutch cocoa powder)

To remove seeds from the vanilla bean, run the tip of a pairing knife lengthwise down the center of the bean to expose the seeds, split the bean into 2 halves and place skin side down on a cutting board. Using the dull edge of a knife, run the knife down the center of each pod to remove the seeds. In a small bowl, use your fingertips to thoroughly combine the vanilla seeds and sugar so that no clumps remain.

Note: The empty vanilla pods can be utilized to infuse various liquids or added to a jar of sugar to create vanilla-scented sugar.

Using an electric mixer, beat butter and vanilla sugar together on medium high until thoroughly combined. Beat in the egg whites one at a time. Lower the speed and add the flour until just combined. Do not over mix.

Cover bowl and refrigerate for at least 1 hour prior to use.
This recipe will produce more than what is required for one dish. I like to portion the batter and freeze for later use.

White Chocolate Sauce

This dessert sauce has a perfect consistency for garnishing many dishes. This is a staple in my pantry that I keep readily available in a squeeze bottle to decorate plates for service.

¾ cup water
¼ cup light corn syrup or glucose syrup
½ vanilla bean
16 ounces (454 grams) white chocolate, pieces, or callets* (preferably coverture chocolate*)

Add water and syrup into a small heavy-bottomed saucepan.

To remove seeds from the halved vanilla bean, run the tip of a paring knife lengthwise down the center of the bean to expose the seeds, split the bean into two halves and place skin side down on a cutting board. Using the dull edge of a knife, run the knife down the center of each pod to remove the seeds.

Place the pod and seeds into the water. Heat mixture to a low simmer on medium heat. Remove from the heat and stir the white chocolate into the liquid until thoroughly incorporated. When cooled, transfer sauce to a squeeze bottle and refrigerate for up to 2 weeks.

Yields 1¼ cups

Antigua Black Pineapple

Glossary & Index

The glossary is designed in alphabetical order.
Here you will find definitions of certain
ingredients and cooking techniques that are
marked with an asterisk throughout the book.

The index is listed in alphabetical order, allowing
ease when searching for a certain recipe or ingredient.
The recipe theme is also listed (for example,
soups, salads, pork, or lobster).

Agar Agar: red algae readily available in powder or flake form. It acts as a setting agent very similar to gelatin only it has stronger setting properties so less of the agent is needed. Agar agar is vegan friendly.

Al Dente: an Italian expression which translates "to the tooth." This method refers to food that is cooked to the point where it offers a slight resistance.

Bangkok Blend: a Thai seasoning mixture combined of the following dry ingredients: sweet peppers, garlic, ginger, black pepper, galangal, hot peppers, lemon grass, basil, and cilantro. This seasoning can be purchased online from Penzeys Spices.

Bavarian Seasoning: a German seasoning mixture combined of the following ingredients: crushed brown mustard, rosemary, garlic, thyme, bay leaf, and sage. This seasoning can be purchased online from Penzeys Spices.

Biscoff Cookies: thin caramel-flavored wafers full of spice that have a wonderful snap and are very versatile.

Bloom: the process by which gelatin softens and swells when added to water, enabling the granules to dissolve smoothly when heated.

Bouquet Garni: term for a bunch of herbs, either tied together or wrapped in cheesecloth, and submerged into sauces, stocks, soups, or stews to infuse additional flavor.

Boursin Cheese: brand of Gournay cheese originally produced in France. It has a soft, creamy texture similar to whipped cream cheese and comes in a variety of flavors.

Brunoise: a mixture of various vegetables that have been cut into a small dice and are usually cooked in butter.

Buffalo Mozzarella: or Mozzarella Di Bufala is the most valued fresh mozzarella. It is made from a combination of water, buffalo's milk, and cow's milk. You can purchase this product in most specialty grocery stores or at fine Italian delicatessens.

Bulgur Wheat: a tasty grain derived from wheat berries. This grain has a lovely, light nutty flavor, is very easy to use, high in nutrients, and can be used to substitute rice in a pilaf.

Butcher's Twine: also known as cooking or kitchen twine, is a 100% cotton string that is used for various applications in the kitchen such as trussing roast chicken or stuffed loins.
Note: Butcher's twine is not edible and must be discarded prior to service.

Calcium Chloride: an inorganic compound used for spherfication. I purchase this product online from Modernist Pantry.

Calcium Lactate: a salt used for spherification. I purchase this product online from Modernist Pantry.

Callets: chocolate disks praised by chocolatiers for their uniform size and ideal crystalline structure. These are my preference when working with chocolate.

Caster Sugar: extra fine granulated sugar, ideal for making meringues and sweetening cold liquids due to its rapid dissolving power.

Charnushka: seed found in traditional Indian, Lebanese, Turkish, and Serbian dishes. Also known as Nigella or black cumin seeds, they have a sharp flavor with hints of thyme. It is a wonderful addition to vegetable dishes or as a topping for bread and savory pastries.

Cheesecloth: also known as muslin, is a 100% cotton fabric that is woven in either fine or course weave. A very useful kitchen tool, it is most commonly used to strain liquids, wrap rolled meats, or enclose herbs in a bouquet garni.

Chiffonade: French phrase that means "made of rags." It is a description of a style of cut, which refers to thin strips or shreds of vegetables or herbs.

Cipollini Onions: small variety of onion from the bulb of the grape hyacinth plant. They can normally be found in Italian specialty shops.

Coconut Cream: a milk-like product made by soaking grated coconut, water, and milk of the coconut. It is available by the can in the Asian food section of most grocery stores. Do not confuse it with canned "cream of coconut," which is thick, sweet, and used in desserts or drinks.

Colander: a perforated bowl used to strain items from liquid.

Consommé: clarified meat or fish broth that is packed with flavor.

Coverture Chocolate: high-grade patisserie chocolate famed for its higher percentage of cocoa butter. The additional cocoa butter, combined with the proper tempering, gives the chocolate additional sheen and a firmer "snap" when broken, making it ideal for any chocolate use.

Crab Boil Mix: combination blend of the following ingredients: yellow and brown mustard seeds, allspice, coriander, cloves, bay leaf, ginger, black pepper, chili pepper, dill seed, and caraway seed. This seasoning can be purchased online from Penzeys Spices.

Crème Fraîche: a thick cream made from heavy cream and the addition of an acid such as lemon, buttermilk, sour cream, or yogurt. It is similar to sour cream.

Cryovac Machine: also known as a vacuum sealer, is a small kitchen appliance that removes the air from a food-grade plastic bag and seals it using a heated strip.

Deglaze: a method where you use a small amount of liquid to remove and dissolve the brown bits that remain in a sauté pan after the food and excess fat has been removed. The liquid used is usually stock or wine and becomes the base for an accompanying sauce or gravy to the cooked food.

Demi-Glace: a rich sauce that usually complements red meat. It is a reduction of brown stock and espagnole sauce.

Double Boiler: a saucepan with a detachable upper bowl or sleeve that is used to gently heat liquids or temper chocolate using steam.

Duck Confit: French specialty derived from an ancient method of preserving meat. The duck, usually the thighs and legs, are salted and then slowly cooked in duck fat. The meat is then cooled and left in the fat for preservation. It can be stored in the fridge for long periods of time, up to six months.

Dust: to lightly coat with a powdery ingredient such as cocoa, flour, or sugar.

Emulsify: to combine two or more immiscible (non-combining) liquids together. For example: oil and water, this method is done by slowly adding one ingredient to the other while whisking vigorously.

Ferrero Rocher: a popular small, round chocolate made with hazelnut and wafers produced by the famous Italian chocolatier, Ferrero.

Filo or Phyllo: paper-thin pastry, originating in Greece that is used for wrapping both sweet and savory ingredients.

Foie Gras: the liver of a duck or goose that has been fattened, normally by being force-fed. It is considered a delicacy in most countries and prized for its rich, buttery, delicate flavor.

Ghee: clarified butter primarily used in Indian and Asian cuisine.

Herbes de Provence: mixture of dried herbs commonly used in the south of France. The combination includes: basil, fennel seed, lavender, marjoram, rosemary, sage, savory, and thyme.

Jerk Seasoning: a dry seasoning blend that originated in Jamaica. It usually consists of chili, thyme, cinnamon, ginger, allspice, cloves, garlic, and onion. It can be rubbed directly on the ingredient or blended with liquid to create a spicy marinade.

Kombu: one of the main ingredients in dashi, a popular Japanese broth. Kombu is a long dark brown seaweed that is dried and packaged for later use.

Macerate: means "to soften" or "to steep;" for example, soaking an ingredient in a liquid in order to infuse it with the liquid's flavor.

Mandolin: a kitchen utensil that uses a variety of blades to cut firm foods with uniformity and precision.

Mahi Mahi: also known as dolphin fish or dorado, it has firm flesh with a pale pink hue. A fast fish which can grow up to 45 pounds, mahi mahi is a tasty catch and best when prepared simple and fresh.

Massaman Curry Paste: a southern Thai curry paste consisting of chili, garlic, lemongrass, shallots, ginger, cardamom, clove, cinnamon, coriander, cumin, cilantro, peanuts, nutmeg, turmeric, and salt. My preferred pre-prepared paste is *Mae Ploy*.

Melon Baller: a diverse kitchen utensil, originally used to create a perfect ball of melon (hence the name). It can be used to form a ball shape in numerous products.

Microplane: commercial name for a "rasp grater": a fine, very sharp grater primarily used to zest citrus, grate hard cheese, nutmeg, garlic and ginger, or shave chocolate.

Mise en place: is the preparation of dishes and ingredients prior to service.

Miso Paste: a traditional flavoring paste in Japanese food made from fermented soybeans that have been mixed with salt and a mold called koji, which is also used to make sake. Its pungent flavor is ideal for various dishes.

Mitchell Street Seasoning: this seasoning blend is a combination of salt, Tellicherry black pepper, paprika, sugar, garlic, onion, dill weed, lemon peel, cardamom, citric acid, natural smoke flavor, and allspice. It is very flavorful and can be purchased online from Penzeys Spices.

Montreal Steak Seasoning: this seasoning blend is a combination of salt, garlic, coriander, black pepper, cayenne pepper flakes, and dill seed. This seasoning can be purchased in most supermarkets.

Old Bay Seasoning: is a spice mixture that originated over sixty years ago in the Chesapeake Bay region of the United States. It adds a wonderful flavor to many seafood, poultry, and meat dishes and is a combination of salt, paprika, mustard, ancho, celery, black and red pepper, dill, caraway, allspice, ginger, cardamom, thyme, bay, mace, cinnamon, savory, and cloves. This seasoning can be purchased in most supermarkets.

Oyster Sauce: a concentrated reduction of oyster brine and soy sauce used widely in Asia. It imparts richness to a dish without overpowering its flavor. You can purchase this product in specialty Asian markets or in the Asian section of most supermarkets.

Ovenproof: term for a utensil or cooking container that can withstand heat up to 500°F (260°C) making it appropriate for placing into the oven.

Pacojet: a professional Swiss kitchen appliance that creates, with a patented micro purée process called "pacotizing," perfectly formed, smooth textured sorbet, ice cream, sauces, and soups.

Panko: a type of breadcrumb used in Japanese cooking as a coating for various foods to be fried. The crumbs are much coarser than conventional American breadcrumbs and create a crunchier crust. You can find this product in Asian markets and most supermarkets.

Parmesan-Reggiano Cheese: the preeminent Parmesan cheese in the marketplace and only produced in the provinces of Bologna, Mantua, Modena, or Parma in Italy. By Italian law, all Parmesan cheeses produced outside this region cannot bare its name. Made from skimmed or partially skimmed cow's milk, this straw-colored granular cheese has a rich, sharp flavor and is typically aged longer than other Parmesans.

Pink Curing Salt: a salt comprised of sodium nitrite and table salt that is primarily used in the preparation of sausage and cured meats. The pink color is added to differentiate the salt from regular table salt and the sodium nitrite is added to inhibit bacteria growth. I purchase this product online from the Modernist Pantry.

Polenta: a side dish made from cornmeal and originating in northern Italy. It can be served in a variety of ways: soft, firm, chilled, fried, or pan-seared, and sometimes has the addition of cheese.

Prepared Horseradish: grated raw horseradish root usually combined with vinegar and salt.

Quenelle: a small chicken, fish, or vegetable dumpling bound with egg and formed by pressing a spoonful of the ingredient against the bowl of a second spoon to form an oval. It is also a term used to describe a sweet such as ice cream, sorbet, or mousse formed into an oval using the same technique.

Red Lentil: also known as Egyptian lentils, these lentils are small, reddish orange in color and without a seed coat. Rich in vitamins and calcium, easy to use and delicious, they are commonly used for traditional Indian dhal. Find them in Middle Eastern and East Indian Markets.

Ribbons (vegetable): vegetables that are cut lengthwise into thin slices using a mandolin or vegetable peeler.

Rice Wine Vinegar: vinegar distilled from rice grains that is milder than average vinegar and used primarily in Japanese cuisine.

Roux: a combination of flour and fat that is cooked over low heat and used to thicken soups and sauces. There are three forms of roux: white, blond, and brown. The type of roux depends on the length of time in which it is cooked. Brown, which has been cooked for the longest period of time, has a distinct nutty flavor.

Score: to make shallow cuts, typically in the shape of a diamond, into the surface of foods, such as meat or seafood.

Sift: to pass dry ingredients through a mesh sifter or strainer to remove debris and integrate more air into the ingredient.

Silpat: thin, flexible, non-stick silicone mat that comes in a variety of sizes to fit most baking sheets and provides a reusable nonstick surface for baking.

Simple Syrup: a solution of sugar and water that is cooked over low heat until sugar is dissolved and liquid is clear, and then boiled for a minute or so to reach a syrup consistency. The syrup can be thin (3 parts water to 1 part sugar) medium (2 parts water to 1 part sugar) or thick (equal sugar and water). They are used as the basis for candies, soaking cakes, glazing baked goods, or poaching and preserving.

Sinew: a thin pearlescent membrane found on meat and fish that becomes chewy when cooked and initiates the flesh to curl.

Skim: to remove solids from the surface of a liquid.

Slurry: a mixture of 2 parts liquid and 1 part cornstarch used as a thickening agent for a variety of applications.

Sodium Alginate: a brown algae extraction used as one of the main ingredients in producing molecular caviar and spheres. The product also acts as an emulsifier, increasing the viscosity of liquid. I purchase this product online from Modernist Pantry.

Sodium Citrate: is the sodium salt of citric acid and is used as an acidity regulator. It also has properties that aid in emulsifying oils. I purchase this product online from Modernist Pantry.

Sriracha: a Thai chili sauce made of ground chili, vinegar, sugar, garlic, and salt.

Star Anise: a small, brown, star-shaped spice that is dried and used whole or ground.

Sweet Chili Sauce: an Asian condiment made of chili peppers, vinegar, salt, sugar, and spices.

Tamari: a dark sauce made from soybeans, which is similar to soy sauce, but thicker and more robust in flavor.

Tamarind Concentrate: a paste made from the tropical fruit pod of the tamarind tree. A black robust paste, it is used as a marinade or to flavor a variety of culinary dishes.

Tellicherry Pepper: a superior variety of Indian pepper known for its richness and full-bodied flavor.

Tempering: a cooking method that allows an ingredient to gradually increase in temperature to keep it from curdling or separating.

Thai Fish Sauce: an Asian condiment made from fish or small krill that have been salted and fermented for up to two years.

Thai Red Curry Paste: The paste consists of chilis, coriander, lemongrass, black pepper, galangal, kaffir lime leaves, cilantro, shrimp paste, and salt. My preferred pre-prepared paste is *Mae Ploy.*

Torchon: translates as "dish towel" in French and is the original term referring to a cooking technique whereby a kitchen towel is used to wrap around the product that is being cooked. Today it is also used in reference to the cylindrical shape and cooking method.

Vegetable Oil: liquid oils derived from plants. I prefer to use high smoke point vegetable oils that have a mild, almost neutral, taste. For example: safflower, grape seed, peanut, or avocado oils.

Vidalia Onion: is one of the sweetest and juiciest sweet onion varieties. Grown in Vidalia, Georgia, the onion is large and a favorite for roasting or making traditional French onion soup.

Worcestershire Sauce: a pungent sauce, developed in India but first produced in Worcester, England. It contains molasses, vinegar, sugar, salt, onions, anchovies, garlic, cloves, tamarind, and chili pepper

Inside the Whale's Tale, Norman's Cay,
Exuma Island's, Bahamas

ABOUT THE EDITOR

Virginia Lee, mentor and mother of Chef Elizabeth Lee, is the author of the Flavours line of guidebook and cookbooks with her sister, Elaine Elliot. Together, they have produced many cookbooks that specialize in Canadian and coastal maritime cuisine. She is a native Nova Scotian and divides her time between Lower Canard, Nova Scotia, and North Palm Beach, Florida.

ABOUT THE DESIGNER AND PHOTOGRAPHER

Warren East, partner of Elizabeth, is a multi-talented captain, sous-chef, product designer, photographer, drone pilot, and artist. Although Warren's foundations in yachting were planted at an early age, his entry into the commercial sector began in 1994 when he joined the UK Sailing Academy to achieve the licenses required to operate larger charter yachts. His yachting experience has progressed through the years positioning him as an expert in most elements of the yachting profession.

Throughout his career Warren has received a Maritime Coastguard Agency Master 3000 captain's license, Marshal Islands Endorsement for yachts up to 3000 GT and Padi Divemaster certificate. He has completed more than 400 successful charters in destinations worldwide since 1995 and has logged more than 450,000 nautical miles at sea.

Warren has also assisted with the sale and project management of five custom built, alloy super catamarans, and in 2005 he began his own boutique charter yacht company, East Yachts Limited. Warren's goal with East Yachts is to provide his clients with a professional service in every facet of the yachting industry. His network of contacts worldwide ensure that East Yacht's clients are taken care of wherever their adventures take them.

ABOUT THE CHEF AND AUTHOR

Chef Elizabeth Lee's passions lovingly revolve around culinary arts and the ocean. A Canadian, Elizabeth was born and raised in Nova Scotia and professionally trained in culinary arts on the Pacific coast in British Columbia, Canada. Chef Elizabeth graduated with honors and a Culinary Arts degree from the University of the Okanagan in Kelowna, British Columbia, in 2001. Immediately after graduation, she worked as the sous-chef at a fine dining, five star Italian restaurant in Whistler, British Columbia, Canada's largest ski resort.

In 2003, Elizabeth moved to the yachting sector, leaving the mountains and northern climate for the sunny Caribbean. It is with thanks to her sister, Katie Lee, that her eyes were opened to a career on the high seas, sailing in many of the world's most beautiful places on prestigious yachts and cooking for the rich and famous.

After three years in the yachting industry, Elizabeth teamed up with Captain/photographer Warren East, her partner in "life and love."

Elizabeth quickly transitioned into a renowned chef within the industry, winning various chef competitions in the Caribbean and abroad, including Concours de Chef, Best Chef of the Year, BVI, Turkey, and third place in the Antigua Chef Competition.

Together, Warren and Elizabeth have logged 250,000 miles traveling the world on yachts to destinations in North America, the Caribbean, Trans-Atlantic, Mediterranean, and the Near East. Elizabeth's direct access to the culture and gastronomy from around the world has influenced her food in myriad ways, all of which have been infused into the recipes showcased in this book.

Elizabeth believes in the evolving science of gastronomy and specializes in avant-garde, sous vide, molecular gastronomy, nouvelle, Pacific Rim, and fusion cuisines. Her expertise in creating exquisite flavors and artistic presentations is renowned throughout the industry.

When Elizabeth first came into my life in 2006, I would never have imagined the amazing life story that was about to unfold. Within days of her arrival aboard *S/Y Wonderful* she had already 'wowed' me with one of the best meals I had ever eaten and she didn't stop there. Over the years, I have listened to countless charter guests and yacht owners claim they just ate the best meal of their lives. Many even repeating the claim with their next meal. That says a lot about Elizabeth's formula, which has been 100% consistent since day one. An admirable feat.

It has been an honor to work alongside Elizabeth on this great journey to complete her book, *MADE WITH LOVE*. To be able to share in the joy of her success is wonderful to me.

Elizabeth, you are amazing.
Your loving husband,

Warren.